STUMBLING ACROSS THE OBVIOUS

THE RIDDLE OF CHANGE IN CORPORATIONS

HENRIK GRUBER

CO-AUTHORED BY **ALEXANDER BIRKE**

CONTENTS

FOREWORD

HENRIK AND I MET ABOUT FIVE YEARS AGO AND BONDED OVER our passion for agile methodology and mindsets, as well as our shared vision for improving things in this world. Without getting too corny about it, you might say we love the idea of making this world a better place. In the intervening years, we have spoken a lot about the things that surprise us—problems that seem obvious to us, at least. And we've spent a lot of time discussing how we might be able to help. Eventually, we came to the conclusion that we would not be able to save the world, in either of the settings in which we are engaged. But that should not stop us from trying our best.

Each of us can look back on about twenty years of work experience, most of it gained in the role of an internal or external consultant. Even just within the last five years, we have each visited, worked with, and seen between 50-70 companies. All of these visits fall under the general description of "fixing some problems". This entails observing, analysing, consulting, coaching and training clients all over Europe. Across all of these scenarios with different companies, we have seen more similarities than you might expect and about which we are reporting here.

When you hear that we are consultants, you might picture two suit-wearing, PowerPoint-rocking persons. While we can and we do, this is not all we are about. We are deeply concerned about helping people to improve their workplace. That's what drives us. As most people spend a considerable proportion of their lifetimes at work, we want to empower them to carry out meaningful projects with motivated teams that create successful products. For us, change is omnipresent. We help people to question and change the way they think, behave and work. We are well aware that, as outsiders, our powers are limited. Moreover, we don't presume we have the magical ability to change people overnight.

We are extremely interested in people, in what makes them tick and how they are driven to solve their problems. We combine this with a passion to use known methods, models and frameworks to change something for the better. We are not afraid to get our hands dirty; PowerPoint is just the start of the journey. We are role models, coaches and teachers, working one to one or with whole teams. We believe that taking a firm yet gentle, people-centred approach to change will lead to a cultural shift.

You may wonder why we haven't simply included prescribed solutions for each of our stories. As you are well aware, our industry is filled with complexity. Even when things appear to be straightforward, there are countless variables for dozens of factors that all influence applications and outcomes. Usually, the most important factor is the people involved. Although there are no easy answers, we want to share with you what has helped us in these cases. We hope that they will be as helpful for you as they were for us.

—A.B.

PREFACE

O N A SUNNY THURSDAY MORNING, I WAS ENJOYING A HOTEL breakfast with my girlfriend, Julia, in Freiburg, Breisgau. She was there for a language certification, and I was there to accompany her and support her by any means. You would have thought I'd try to reduce her pre-exam jitters, perhaps by making some light conversation and exchanging a few words in French, and generally not stressing her out by causing her to think about anything other than the exam. Well, quite the opposite happened. As we sat at the breakfast table, I became very agitated about my work. Specifically, the people and complications I commonly have to deal with, and the whole litany of things I am forced to explain again and again—everything contained within these pages. I am a consultant who work for clients, most of them within the field of information technology, on large-scale projects. What this really means is that I generally incite company changes that affect around 800 people. I'm sure you can imagine exactly how popular this makes me.

Julia listened carefully and helped me understand why I was so frustrated. Our conversation inspired me to write this book. For years, I had been stumbling across the obvious. Although it always was right there in front of me, it only became apparent in that moment. I realised that what was obvious to me might not yet be to others. Some of the riddles in these pages may bear a striking resemblance to the ones you have faced or are currently facing. I hope my words will help you to see things from a new vantage point, from which you'll be able to view things more clearly and never take anything for granted. It is my intention and the ambition of this book to guide you towards new shores.

—H.G.

INTRODUCTION

WHILE PART OF OUR JOB IS HELPING COMPANIES TO CHANGE for the better, we are always learning from them and learning together with them. By walking you down the paths we've taken, we might be able to help you to avoid making the mistakes we have made ourselves or observed others making in the past. In some cases, that mistake is inaction. While failing to act is not generally thought to be as bad as making a mistake, the consequences can be just as dire.

No matter the situation in which you find yourself, this book will show you that you are not alone. Rather than shying away from tough decisions or difficult conversations, it is essential to engage with others to try to understand where they're coming from and give them options for the future. Keep in mind that some people may need consistent coaching and guidance. Everything we do should bear fruit. We should strive for positive change. This decade is framed by constant change. Nothing seems to last for as long as it did in the past, and the future will be more different than we can possibly imagine.

Let us solve the riddle of change in organisations by talking about how they function and what really makes them tick. By demystifying their processes and structures, we can be more mature and creative in solving problems and overcoming obstacles. In the words of Ralph Waldo Emerson, the American transcendentalist poet and philosopher: "Knowledge is when you learn something new every day. Wisdom is when you let something go every day." Just as it is essential to acquire new skills and adopt fresh perspectives, we must also surrender the unconstructive patterns, assumptions and hierarchies that obstruct positive change if we wish to make a real difference in this world.

In these pages, we present the most striking stories, observations and impressions we've encountered over the course of our professional career thus far, in the hope that they will inspire and inform you and position you to make a huge leap forward.

This book will be valuable for those who are new to consultancy and are seeking some early insight, and for those who may have been in this profession for some time and are seeking to broaden their horizons or rejuvenate their work lives. Whether you work in or lead a start-up or a company in the tech, finance, legal, consumer goods or government sector, you are likely always striving to enhance your organisation's cohesion, size, structure and perspective. This book was written for people of all walks of life who wish to wake up every morning and feel inspired.

When I started writing this book, I was considering all kinds of different approaches. Most books on this topic seem to focus on how to do everything right or how to do everything wrong. They either reel out a list of products and projects that have failed tragically (or laughably, as the case may be) or provide a step-by-step guide to achieving greatness or building a monstrously successful product. I decided to combine both approaches and to add another element. I provide real case studies—true stories and not textbook examples—which give an honest impression and tell a story to which most readers will relate. I'll be reflecting upon (and venting about) some situations I have seen playing out repeatedly throughout the course of my career and finding out what we can learn from them

Specifically, this book will focus on mad situations I've observed and examine them through a constructively critical lens.

This book is divided into three sections. In **Part A: CONUN-DRUMS,** I will airlift you right into various real-life situations and you will see them playing out in glorious, gory detail right before your eyes. You may ask, as I did: *Am I dreaming? Is this actually happening?* Some of these cases will seem so far removed from reality that you might suspect that I am exaggerating. I almost wish I was, but I can assure you that this is not the case. I'd like to process what happened at the time, to examine how I and others dealt with matters, and to come up with ideas of how to approach them if they happen to occur again. As you might have guessed, I strongly believe they will.

Most of the case studies are followed with a section titled **What to consider or try now**. This is a list of recommended topics to re-search and proactive strategies and techniques you can set in mo-tion straight away to address the issues we've discussed. This will ultimately be more helpful to you than simply prescribing a solution or a step-by-step guide.

Part B: DIFFERENT PERSPECTIVES contains a different point of view. Actually several. I invited guest writers to share their view on change in organisations. Read through these astonishing chapters to feel inspired. In case you want to reach out to the writ-ers directly, find their names at the beginning of each chapter.

Part C: EPIPHANIES comprises takeaway guides to help your future projects to succeed. We hope that sharing our experience and making concrete suggestions will help you to recognise unproduc-tive patterns, avoid potential pitfalls, and overcome obstacles. If we can anticipate and eradicate these from our work environment, we can focus our attention on the other surprises that are bound to pop up along the way. Come back to this part of the book whenever you need inspiration.

PART A:
CONUNDRUMS

T HIS SECTION COULD HAVE BEEN TITLED *Things People Say on Projects Destined to Struggle and/or Fail.* Each statement encapsulates an attitude or mindset that underlies problematic scenarios I have encountered more than once.

You can take each case study and target these issues within your project. Or, proactively work on them within your environment so as to never let them play out for real. I present these case studies without providing hard-and-fast answers, because every situation contains unique elements that require a slightly different approach. Ultimately, you will have to finetune the solution for each situation, but as long as you can recognise the most broadly occurring patterns, you will always be prepared.

01 | WE ARE ALL CUSTOMERS

W HEN CLIENTS COME TO ME AND SAY, *I HAVE A PROJECT FOR you,* that's music to my ears. Projects are awesome—they give you focus, a sense of purpose, a plan. You establish your strategy, make a few calls, and get all of the right people involved. At some point in time, most likely right at the outset, you fix a deadline. You set out on a certain course with tangible outcomes. You put a plan into action, and, within a reasonable span of time, you'll start to be able to see results. What could be better than that? In theory, it doesn't seem all that complicated.

> 66
>
> In theory, practise and theory are the same. In practise, they are not.

Then, reality sets in. Before you know it, piles of work are being thrown at you, and you feel like you might drown. Conflicts arise and multiply. Who will take the initiative to lead the project, to be in charge, to bear responsibility and accountability? Accountability is the burning baton no one wants to touch unless the project turns out to be a resounding success. We all love the feeling of achieving our goals; of receiving thanks and appreciation; of having accomplished something truly worthwhile. But what does it take to get there?

Before we get started, I want to share something I read in Tim Ferris' *Tools of Titans*, which has stayed with me:

> If there are stories that make you angry, look deeper into them, because it could be that precisely this topic has a deep meaning for you which you should maybe investigate.[1]

I NEVER MET A CUSTOMER - WHY SHOULD I? IT'S THE COMPANY I SERVE, NOT THEM.

I have encountered this attitude more times than I can count. As a case in point, I'd like to examine a particular project and view it from the perspectives of the customer and the corporation, respectively.

I was appointed to take over the guidance of a few teams (comprising roughly one hundred people) involved in implementing a new software product. The project entailed streamlining the workflow for a few thousand customer service employees whose roles required them to integrate various IT applications and manual processes. Apparently, these customer service agents had a wealth of intrinsic knowledge and therefore this had to be transferred into software; however, no one had anticipated the range of individual behaviours and working processes.

Let's first look at this from the customer's viewpoint. A customer is primarily interested in receiving excellent service and quick results. At this point I'd like to introduce Carlo, who will be accompanying us on our journey through these pages.

[1] Ferris, Tim. *Tools of Titans: The Tactics, Routines, and Habits of Billionaires, Icons, and World-Class.* Vermilion, 2016

Carlo represents our model user, client or customer of the product or software to be used. Whenever we are supposed to have customer contact (and even when, sadly, such contact does not take place), Carlo will appear. Carlo is a somewhat emotional and extroverted individual, who is never too shy to state his opinion. Carlo is a man of action—always eager to get things done. Let's see how he fares in the pages to come.

Carlo Customer - Impulsive, extroverted customer. He just loves a smooth service.

A typical use case was that every job applicant must be interviewed by a customer service agent. This process is intended to glean the information needed to match applicants with the position and company for which they are best suited. In this case, Carlo happened to be the hopeful job applicant. The agent gathered various fields of information, including Carlo's name, interests, and spoken languages, and entered these into the relevant forms.

As the company comprises many departments, each having various kinds of application forms to be processed, Carlo was often kept waiting while the customer service agent consulted a colleague who was more knowledgeable about a specific application form. All too often, the colleague they had phoned would have to call upon yet another colleague for assistance with a field with which they were unfamiliar or a text box for which they did not know the context. The longer Carlo had to wait, the more agitated and impatient he grew. He eavesdropped on the conversations between his customer service agent and her other colleagues. The more he heard, the more

> **❝❞**
> Never debate about internal processes in front of a customer.

he began to doubt whether his customer service agent was really capable of helping him. His faith in the company as a whole began to dwindle.

There were countless other ways in which the customer service representatives were forced to waste Carlo's valuable time. The customer service agent, who had already scanned Carlo's driver's license, was then required to scan it again for a different application. As the only scanner was being used by someone else or was temporarily out of use, the agent had to type in an identifying case number, to match it up within the systems.

Carlo discovered this a few days later, when he contacted the company to provide some background information he had forgotten to mention at his previous appointment. When he phoned them, they asked for his identifying case number, which consisted of ten characters comprising a mixture of numbers and letters. He grew incredibly frustrated, and understandably so.

The new software and set of applications were designed to streamline this somewhat Kafkaesque workflow (as well as to address many other issues that I won't list here) to facilitate fast, high quality service. The agents would be able to devote more time and energy to addressing their clients' questions and concerns instead of negotiating the processes, and others would not suffer as Carlo had.

WHAT TO CONSIDER OR TRY NOW

Elemental factors of improving the customer focus in a company are leadership accountability, understanding and using the power of technology / IT, getting rid of siloed company structures and make room for brainstorming, experimenting and innovation.

- **Experiment** with new technologies that provide general solutions to typical problem areas: e.g., artificial intelligence (AI), robotic process automation (RPA), virtual or extended reality (VR, XR), etc.

- **Make** product improvement an interdisciplinary team task, as Toyota did in the early Nineties.[2] Functional people are simply not enough. Incorporate marketing, operations, build & test, engineers, designers, etc. The amount of new ideas might be greater, early discussion and validation happens sooner, which makes up a better fitting product.

- **Ensure** that everyone in your company has a clear picture of who your customers are and how they behave in terms of needs, processes, tools, and so on. While visiting and shadowing are definitely among the best approaches, learning materials, videos and the concept of personas are just as crucial.

- **Provide** interaction channels customers can use to give you feedback and learn. These may include feedback buttons within the application, visible phone numbers and e-mail addresses, and chat groups focused on problems as well as on innovation ideas.

- **Gather** data from your users including personal feedback and data about their product usage behaviours. This is a very easy task for internet applications. Think in terms of "time spent on a page" (complexity and understandability of the page) versus "pages loaded to solve a need" (how many steps or back-and-forths is required before task is achieved). If you're interested in modern product development methods, you may wish to check out the work of Marty Cagan.

---

[2] Takeuchi, Hirotaka and Ikujiro Nonaka."The New New Product Development Game." *Harvard Business Review.* From the Jan. 1986 review. https://bit.ly/3mGvV8j

ALL LARGE COMPANIES HAVE THEIR COMPLEXITIES.
THERE IS NOTHING YOU CAN DO ABOUT IT.

Many companies will defend their fatal flaws with statements like the one above. The case study involving Carlo exemplifies how the systems that have been installed for purpose of facilitating smooth operations may end up stunting the progress of the corporations they are meant to support. Carlo's primary concern was to search for a new job, and the company was supposed to assist him in this endeavour. However, the customer service agent was too busy figuring out the company's internal complex processes to be able to attend to his needs.

Some organisations become so stuck in their ways that they lose all critical awareness. Or, they simply forget to reflect upon or scrutinise the status quo. By failing to see their shortcomings, they miss every opportunity to simplify or expedite their processes and increase productivity. All too often, I have found myself asking: *Why doesn't anyone take the initiative to do something to help this company stop wasting its employees' time and intellectual capacity?* After working with many such companies, I became inspired to write down my observations and to come up with some suggestions for how to cut through all this noise and create space for something new and fresh.

Problems arise when a system requires its users to spend so much time and mindpower navigating the system itself that it ceases to support their innovation, teamwork, and ability to function to the best of their potential. Hierarchies, boundaries, and the delegation of tasks are instated with the aim of enabling employees to focus on their given tasks, but when these delineations become too rigid and constricting, they form barriers that isolate employees and inhibit collaborative processes, serving instead to prevent them from working together effectively toward their common goal. Even in cases where an individual within such an organisation identifies an issue and raises a suggestion for how to overcome it, they may be too secluded to get the support needed to successfully implement it even within their own department, not to mention across the whole organisation.

Within the aforementioned corporation, employees were neither invited nor encouraged to improve or innovate. They were given a task and expected to solve it within a certain amount of time. Their job contracts prohibited them from crossing department borders, inviting others to share opinions, and so forth. Why? They were simply not involved in any improvements being driven by other departments. Furthermore, their contracts didn't allow them to deviate from the task at hand. No bonus, pay rise nor any type of sustainable incentive was offered to employees for doing anything other than solving their cases, completing tasks more quickly or making fewer mistakes.

An article published on the Innovation Asset Group's blog identified nine key contributing factors that hinder internal innovation processes.[3] Let's go over these points and how we might be able to address them.

1 | **Employees aren't empowered to innovate.** Whether employees have the permission and latitude to innovate is a systemic issue that stems from the company's structure; however, it can still be addressed via more effective management and leadership.

2 | **Employees aren't incentivised to innovate.** Employees should be encouraged to seek out ways to fruitfully involve themselves and they should be acknowledged and rewarded for do-

[3] Playford, Brendan. "9 Challenges Hindering Innovation in Your Organization." Decipher™ 9 June 2016. https://bit.ly/3iZOcgs

ing so. This provides positive reinforcement and inspires others to innovate as well.

3 | **Lack of an innovation strategy.** Ask yourself the following questions and implement a clear strategy: In which areas is it worth innovating? What is the company actually seeking? What is deemed worth looking into?

4 | **Innovation is centralised within one functional group.** Employees may feel that innovation has been delegated to another group, and therefore they should not innovate at all. This results in what I call Not Invented Here Syndrome. The very existence of centralised groups, regardless of how they actually behave, may create the sense that innovation should take place elsewhere. Every unit should be encouraged to innovate no matter what their individual job title or team's function may be.

5 | **Lack of collaboration.** Modular systems (in which one team does requirement analysis, another team builds the product, and yet another team operates it, and other teams then market and sell it) tend to create silos, which serve as barriers to innovation. When each unit's purpose of existence is isolated from those of the other units, in the long run, they will each forge their own identities and optimise only themselves. You have to organise these units to share a unifying identity, so that they don't lose sight of the overarching purpose of creating one product or service together. As every unit holds pieces of information that will help them to innovate and enhance the product or service, they must be encouraged to constantly interact and communicate so they can put these pieces together.

6 | **Lack of diversity.** In the short term, this can be addressed by applying Toyota's interdisciplinary approach, which, a

we've mentioned, involves intermixing individuals who embody a diverse range of skills and expertise. You can take this a step further by bringing together individuals with various personality types or backgrounds. Lack of diversity tends to arise as a symptom of hierarchical structures and processes, so you will need to closely examine these issues within your organisation and do some restructuring to prevent this from being an ongoing issue.

7 | **Complacency and resistance to change.** This is caused by the success of current product offerings. When your products are successful, it may seem unnecessary and undesirable to innovate, particularly as innovation tends to bring with it some period of disruption that may affect the core of the company and negatively impact the current cash cow. Keeping in mind your product lifecycles and investment horizons can help you to stay motivated to distribute attention and effort towards all areas. Whether it was Ginsberg, Faulkner, Chekhov or someone else who first said "Kill your darlings", this is good advice across the board. Your favourite invention, which you may have built at a more innocent and hopeful point in your career and nurtured for many years, eventually becomes a part of you. While you know it is likely not perfect, you are too emotionally attached to it to be able to see where there is room for improvement. In a larger sense, this might be a change management issue that needs to be dealt with by creating a sense of urgency, e.g., from market pressure. In a smaller setting, you may want to invite people from outside to workshop it with you or place yourself in someone else's shoes to form an objective critique.

8 | **Lack of connection and empathy with your customers.** Unless you really listen to your customers, you will not understand what they really need (which may be different from what they say or think they want) nor how their needs are changing.

If you keep all communication channels open and accessible to your customers, you'll be able to stay inspired and informed to keep innovating products to provide solutions to their problems.

9 | **Failure to measure the right things.** As typical project management metrics focus on efficiency and reaching the set goal, they may not be capable of measuring progress during the U-turns or diversions necessitated during feedback and experimentation loops. Innovation does not follow a straight path, so you need to have an area supported with KPIs with these capabilities.

You might assume that the case we've just discussed is exceptional; I regret to inform you that it isn't. Over the years, I have observed various companies facing very similar challenges. In the pages to come, we will see that while every client's set of circumstances is unique, the individual elements that make up these scenarios are universally encountered. Together we will examine the most commonly experienced pitfalls and challenges and discuss how to avoid or overcome them. Let's see what we can learn from those who've come before us about what it takes to produce something truly beautiful that people love to use.

02 | WHY ARE WE HERE?

W HY ARE WE HERE? FOR ANYONE EXISTING ON THIS EARTH, particularly those of us who are involved in a project, this is the question of ultimate importance. Many of the situations memorialised in these pages were times of existential despair. In these particular projects, I didn't know what I or anyone else was doing there. It felt like we had reached the end of the proverbial road. Somehow, we had all ended up in a ghost town that had been abandoned years ago by most of its inhabitants. We were the last survivors, clinging on for dear life, having long forgotten why we were there.

> Each person should be able to tell you exactly why he or she is on the project.

IT DOESN'T MATTER WHAT WE DO. WE'RE ALL GETTING PAID.

It's time to introduce our next character, Dillon. Dillon is a somewhat disgruntled but nevertheless valued employee. In his youth, he was driven, full of ideas, and eager to learn. Over time,

Dillon became somewhat disillusioned. He stopped dreaming of making his mark in the world. Nowadays, he just does his job. The wellbeing and prosperity of the company is no longer his priority; his focus lies elsewhere.

Dillon Disillusioned - 9-5 employee without ambition. Working-life disgruntled him. He is just in for,   well he forgot.

The title of this chapter can be attributed to Dillon, who has what I call Busy Person Syndrome. The busy person says: *I need to be busy. I'm on the team, but don't ask me why. It's all so frustrating, because no one is accomplishing anything at all. Something around here really has to change, but don't ask me what that is or make me be the one to change.* Dillon cannot tell you what motivates him or what purpose he serves. He simply needs a place to be, and your team happens to be that place.

Dillon brings home the bacon. He gets very frustrated and has regular outbursts, during which he rails against the very inflexible organisation and the status quo. At the end of the year, he typically compiles a long list of his excellent achievements. Occasionally, he receives a raise. Dillon believes his skills are not being appropriately used, as he should have been promoted into management a long time ago, so he often will bully others into letting him play the unofficial team lead, thus revealing his lack of experience. Once Dillon finds that he is in over his head, instead of admitting his shortcomings and trying to acquire the skills he is lacking, he will instead flaunt his incompetency for all to see. Dillon blames his failure on the company, the system, his co-workers—everyone except himself. Dillon is always busy. Partly what keeps him busy is his constant complaining. One has to wonder how much longer he'll be able to keep this up. His behaviour benefits neither his company nor himself.

WHAT TO CONSIDER OR TRY NOW

- **Activity** is not synonymous with output and output is not synonymous with outcome. Instead of asking yourself what you are doing, ask yourself what you are actually producing. Is there an outcome?

- **Ask** yourself whether you are focused on a few key topics or whether you are trying to do ten thousand things in parallel. Narrow things down to the essentials instead of juggling too many balls.

- **While** being seen to be busy conveys a picture of efficiency, staying active is not your target within itself. Taking a smart and lateral approach provides the base for efficient and effective way of working. That's the best way to produce not only output (deliverables) but real outcomes (the bottom line you wanted to affect with the deliverables). Ask yourself whether you fully understand your objectives. Are you working in the smartest and most effective way?

- **Keep** in mind that doing everything the "right" way does not guarantee success. How output translates as an outcome is most often decided by a number of factors, including the environment, the market, and the competition. Sometimes it's just luck that gets you there.

MY JOB CONSISTS PRIMARILY OF PRODUCING PAPERWORK.

Whenever I hear such a statement, I'm surprised. I find it peculiar that someone would ever say the above sentence to another human being. My mind starts to swirl with questions. *Instead of wasting your breath on a sentence that tells me precisely nothing, why wouldn't you describe your company's amazing new product? Is it a tweak of something that already exists or makes it far less complicated to use? Why don't you talk about that instead? Do you truly believe that you go to work every day just to write stuff down? Why wouldn't you search for meaning in what you do?*

Whenever I ask Dillon why he has to carry out so much paperwork, he doesn't talk about communication or record-keeping, as you might expect. He tells me he's doing it because he is required to file x number of words or pages every week. I can appreciate

Everything you do should have a purpose.

that it is necessary to have a paper trail, so that any issues that may arise can be traced back through the documentation. However, it seems to me that unless one bears this specific purpose in mind, one is merely engaging with busywork and fulfilling quotas for their own sake. In this age of software development, the scope and definition of a project is constantly in flux. It seems like a waste of time and energy to devote so much time to nailing everything down. And, especially as much of this paperwork will eventually be stored in separate formats and applications, you have to wonder whether anyone will ever consolidate and utilise all of this information.

Dillon once told me in earnest: *My co-workers and me hardly have time to talk to the development department, because we have so much work to do in order to meet our writing specifications. We have to prioritise this, because this is how the company measures success. With* x y *and* z *documents still outstanding, we can devote only a few hours per week to working on the product itself.* Hearing this sent shivers down my spine.

Wouldn't it make more sense to record the data as succinctly as possible, instead of padding it out with the sole purpose of satisfying an arbitrary word or page count? Someone in the company has decreed that more is better, and everyone unquestioningly follows this rule, especially people like Dillon, who have stopped questioning things. It appears that most people are more concerned with protecting their job security than with enhancing the efficacy of the process.

In his book *The Primes*, Chris McGoff explains that you can change a system only when you work on the system as well as within it.[4] This applies as many things being discussed in the current culture, especially also for learning organisations. These can be seen as investments to future. While this may sound important and reasonable, the tyranny of urgency often exerts a stronger pull.

[4] McGoff, Chris. *The Primes: How Any Group Can Solve Any Problem.* Wiley, 2012. Kindle.

WHAT TO CONSIDER OR TRY NOW

- **Dedicate** space and time for reflecting, learning and working on the system. As set out in the Eisenhower Matrix,[5] if this undertaking must compete against your daily workload, in terms of urgency, it is bound to lose. But while this may not be of the utmost importance at present, in the mid- or long-term, it will be. That's why you need to reserve time for it.

- **Take** a deep dive into Eric Ries' Lean Startup[6] approach or learn about the process of one of the most innovative and award-winning design firms in the world, IDEO[7], if you are interested in modern methods of new product development (often referred to as NPD).

- **Check in** with someone you trust if you feel that a project is floundering. Do they feel the same way? Create alliances to brainstorm the best plan of action. Most likely, the situation is too complex for you to handle alone.

---

[5] "Introducing the Eisenhower Matrix." *Eisenhower.* ® FTL3 Accessed 16 June 2020. https://www.eisenhower.me/eisenhower-matrix/

[6] "The Lean Startup Methodology." The Lean Startup (website). Accessed 24 July 2020. http://theleanstartup.com/principles

[7] "IDEO's Human-Centered Design Process: How to Make Things People Love." User Testing. 4 December 2018. https://bit.ly/3fTTiGQ

I'M JUST FOLLOWING ORDERS.

From my perspective, it is crucial to manage supply and demand. The relationship between supply and demand, and how this is managed, are the sources for many of the problems we have at work.

Let's say you and a friend are making tortellini. Your friend is preparing the dough and squeezing it through a funnel. The dough represents demand. The amount of dough you have available, plus any dough created in the meantime, is to be transformed into pasta by you. You are the supply. As the rate at which you can produce tortellini is limited by the flexibility and speed of your hands, squeezing more dough into the funnel will not speed up the process. The rate of production will increase only as you acquire practice and skill. Your friend must keep feeding the appropriate amount of dough into the funnel. Without enough demand, your funnel will be empty.

Demand typically outweighs supply. Demand creates the pipeline for innovative products.

In business, demand is the concept of requirements, ideas and work that has to be implemented. Demand typically outweighs the realisation capacities (or supply) of a company. Generally speaking, this is a positive thing. New ideas, products and requirements that have not yet been implemented are the reason companies employ us. Work exists, and people then manifest this work into products customers love. There is a restricted amount of capacity at hand, because people can work only for a certain amount of time each day.

Here we come to the root cause. Phil Abernathy described this very precisely when interviewed for a podcast.[8] Though it may seem simpler to ask people to mindlessly follow orders, we should

---

[8] "Three Key Capabilities for Agile Leaders." Business Agility Series. *Accenture SolutionsIQ.* https://bit.ly/310c0bw

strive to separate demand from supply, prioritise appropriately, and give people the freedom to implement something that will make a difference.

People need to be aware of their surroundings, to understand the tasks and the logic underlying how they are to be carried out, and to discover solutions by themselves. Simply telling them what needs to be done creates a situation in which they will need to work faster to keep pace with the ever-growing demand. When forced to work above capacity just so they can deliver faster, people become narrow minded and they try to find shortcuts. In this scenario, it isn't possible to keep an eye on the bigger picture or to keep tabs on the whole system; it is possible only to focus on one's personal goals.

At this point, the ambition is simply to deliver as much and as quickly as possible, since everyone is under stress anyway. There's little to no possibility for creativity or innovation when employees are under time pressure to simply get the job done. As the demand pipeline will (one would hope) never run empty, just pay forward all of the demand and leave others to worry about it. The problem is solved for you as soon as it becomes someone else's problem, so all you need to worry about is clearing your workload. Once it's out of sight, it's out of mind. This kind of behaviour erodes respect within the organisation and is harmful to the collaborative spirit, as people elsewhere in the company will always have the nagging feeling that they may be left holding the bag. Therefore, when you have many people working on specifications and requirements, there should be a proportional number of people assigned to incorporating these into great products.

WHAT TO CONSIDER OR TRY NOW

- **Find** the demarcation line between your demand and supply. It may be worth noting that if you have committed to doing something, you are already in the supply phase.

- **Organise** and manage your demand via a prioritised list.

- **To facilitate** prioritisation, you'll need to understand your economic framework or your value system. To help you identify the big things in life or for the next time, first define what value means to you. Then you'll be able to understand which tasks bear the most importance for you and are allowed to consume your time.

- **Supply** is managed by you or by a team you lead. If this team consists of knowledge workers, it's time to do your research on intentional leadership[9] and situational leadership. As a leader, it's essential to strike a balance between the personality (see DISC or MBTI[10]), acquired and potential competencies, and current knowledge and circumstances of people you're working with. There is no such thing as delegation, self-organisation or happy knowledge workers in your team, unless the leader applies these concepts.

- **Beyond** managing people in supply, there are a few roles to manage the flow in the smartest way possible. Research lean manufacturing system principles, including how to limit parallel work, focus on reducing waste, and so on.

---

[9] "David Marquet: Intent-Based Leadership." The ArmyLeader.co.uk. Accessed 27 July 2020. https://bit.ly/3at9IoD

[10] DISC and MBTI are distinct personality assessment tools. MBTI assumes a stable and continuous personality, while DISC accounts for environmental and experiential impacts on behavior. For more information, see "Using the Myers-Briggs® Instrument with the DISC© Instrument." Psychometrics. https://bit.ly/2Fn5qDv

IT'S FIVE O'CLOCK; TIME TO GO HOME.

Imagine you and your colleagues are engaged in a project that is really coming down to the wire. You and some of your team members are waiting for a particular delivery or handover to take place, so you can start doing your part. You are tying yourself in knots, preparing as much as you can and trying to think of ways to start the work even before you have the parts you need. Then Dillon, the colleague responsible for the aforementioned essential piece of work, utters the words everyone dreads hearing: *Well, it's almost five o'clock. I have to leave.* You stand there in disbelief.

At any other time, this would be a perfectly harmless statement. Under the current circumstances, it harbours resentment and disrespect for others. What Dillon is really saying is: *I don't care. You will find a way. Whatever. See you tomorrow.* When I hear something like this, I am always disappointed and offended. Dillon is telling you bluntly that he has come to work just to punch a clock. He is not your teammate or collaborator. For him, this project has no deeper meaning.

Think back to your college days. I remember studying with my friends in the university library at the weekend. It was fun, working together, firing off questions and answers, collaborating on projects, and experimenting with ideas. We didn't watch the clock. We considered it time well spent, because we understood we were learning something new.

One could argue that work is different from school or university. But, if you love what you do, shouldn't you consider it a kind of freedom to spend time with people who share the same interests, working towards a shared purpose or goal?

WHAT TO CONSIDER OR TRY NOW

In his book Flow: *The Psychology of Optimal Experience,* Hungarian-American psychologist Michael Csikszentmihalyi uses Flow to refer to a personal state in which we are completely absorbed and focused on one dedicated task. This highly focused mental state is the most conducive to efficiency and productivity. He defines the key elements for achieving this state of flow[11] as follows:

- **Clarity** of goals

- **Receiving** immediate feedback, which is intrinsically rewarding

- **Striking** a balance between challenge and skills (similar idea as within situational leadership and intentional / intent-based leadership which were mentioned in the previous chapter)

- **Privacy** with no disturbances and autonomy; feeling in control of the task. When you lack a sense of control over what you do and how you do it, it feels as being controlled by external forces, which commonly leads to frustration and burnout.

[11] Csikszentmihalyi, *Flow: The Psychology of Optimal Experience.* Harper Perennial Modern Classics, 2008.

I'M PAID JUST TO WORK; I'M NOT PAID ENOUGH TO CARE.

I recently watched *American Factory*, a documentary film about a Chinese businessman repurposing a defunct General Motors plant in Ohio to manufacture car windows. Doing so requires bringing in experts from Southeast Asia to retrain some of the local workforce. We see the ambitious, relatively young outsider coming into town with his team of experts, who are prepared to do whatever it takes to make it work. The local recruits, who are slightly older and have more life experience than the people who have come to train them, have to learn to start over. Many of them have families to support; some of them are also pursuing other life goals. Only a few of the locals seem to understand that their town has been given a second chance, and that they have the opportunity to be part of something new and extraordinary. The majority are primarily invested in the workers' union, regular working hours, and anything that might make their lives easier. On the whole, we see a clear division between the Chinese workers, who are prepared to work all night, and the locals, punching out at five o'clock sharp. It's quite uncomfortable to watch.

This reminded me of a project I worked on, in which the team members who were the very last ones to join the project ended up doing most of the work. The team members who had been working longer on the project used the newcomers as the first line of defence by sending them to all of the meetings and workshops and assigning them the most challenging work. By the time the newbies figured out what was happening, it was too late, as they had already spent a considerable amount of time on the project. It wouldn't have made any difference if they had realised sooner, as

> If a few individuals are doing most of the work, eventually this system will tilt.

they were external to the company. There were no internally hired employees, and this encouraged a culture of blame. Some individuals contributed very little, knowing they would benefit from the work put in by others.

Where are the checks and balances or guardrails to prevent this from happening? How can we ensure that everyone contributes to the team and no one is riding on the coattails of others?

WHAT TO CONSIDER OR TRY NOW

- **Assign** roles and responsibilities to all members of your team. I recommend using a responsibility assignment matrix, such as a RACI matrix or linear responsibility chart. Although this doesn't manage personal commitment, it does go some way to set some parameters for equal, transparent and defined distribution of the work.

- **Incorporate** a system that creates transparency for each task, status and outcome. Allowing team members to see how others are performing creates peer pressure, thereby encouraging more engagement. Read up on how best to conduct and facilitate daily standup meetings and obeya rooms and integrate these in your workplace. Collaboration and exchange among team members is key. Be aware that establishing transparency too fast or to much of it at once can put people under stress.

- **Apply** a peering system that connects a rookie to a more experienced team member. The rookie, who sees things with fresh eyes, may spot issues that are not apparent to those who have been there for longer. The more experienced member can provide teaching and guidance, prevent mistakes, and finetune decisions.

I JUST NEED TO HANG IN THERE FOR X
MORE DECADES UNTIL RETIREMENT.

The general retirement age in Europe is sixty-five.[12] Given that most people enter the workforce by their mid-twenties, most of us will pass the halfway point during our early forties. After this point, some people may become less eager to learn, change, experiment and innovate in their careers.

> So much can be accomplished in just a few months. And so little in a decade.

If you found out you had only six months left to live, you might learn to snowboard, cycle across South America or climb to base camp at Mount Everest. Why doesn't the same apply in our professional lives? Why do many of us become complacent instead of feeling inspired to take risks and explore new horizons? Do we, as individuals or as a culture, simply have the wrong attitude to work?

I think it is due to a combination of factors. There is often a shift of focus due to other life goals which become apparent. A person who is raising children or building a home will want to protect their job security, so that they can provide for their families and plan for the future.

Fear is a primary contributing factor. We are afraid of compromising our job security, of failing publicly, or simply of sticking our necks out. Why isn't it worth the risk? Why would we choose stasis and inertia over the possibility to feel excited and create something new? This may be due to deep-seated anger or sheer indifference, or a mixture of the two. Perhaps earlier in our careers we have taken risks and been punished for it or have struggled to gain support from our managers. Perhaps every time we showed some initiative

---

[12] "Ageing and Employment Policies: Statistics on Average Effective Age of Retirement." OECD. Accessed 16 June 2020. https://bit.ly/2E9x32A

we found ourselves running into walls. Eventually, we learned that such attempts resulted only in dissatisfaction and frustration.

Is something inherently lacking in our work environments? Have companies failed to incentivise—have they even actively discouraged—creativity, engagement and innovation? Are the organisations we work for to blame?

So much of the child we were is present in the person we've become. Every person should have a life coach to learn about themselves.

As life expectancy increases, we continue to redefine the concept of ageing. Of course, there is less flexibility in the career spans of professional athletes and dancers practising forms that emphasise raw physical power and brute strength. Those engaged in contact sports, racquet sports, gymnastics and some dance forms (such as ballet) can expect to peak during their twenties and move into coaching, commentating, judging or another career soon afterwards. Meanwhile, long-distance runners, triathletes, golfers, ballroom dancers, yoga practitioners and martial arts experts may peak at any age and are able to extend their professional careers till later in life. Writers, composers, artists, designers, auteurs and academics often see their careers reaching fruition during mid-life and carry on working well into their golden years.

Steve Jobs had accomplished much before he reached the age of twenty-five, but he was past forty when his career reached its prime. In his commencement speech to the graduating class of 2005 at Stanford, he quoted the sign-off message from Stewart Brand's *The Whole Earth Catalog:* "Stay Hungry. Stay Foolish."[13] This was something he had always wished for himself and he wished it for the students, too. It certainly served him well.

[13] Steve Jobs' 2005 Stanford commencement Address. 12 June 2005. Stanford News. https://stanford.io/2E9FECo

Does our culture undervalue learning? We should strive to be eternal students, who keep building knowledge and seeking out new experiences. We should be prepared to take risks, even if it means we might fall on our faces. That's better than standing still. The late John Wooden, a basketball player, three-time All-American, and head basketball coach at UCLA, said: *If you're not making mistakes, you aren't doing anything.* Much can be accomplished later in life. In many cases, this is when one finally has acquired the requisite wisdom, experience, practice, time, and resources to truly excel.

WHAT TO CONSIDER OR TRY NOW

- **Ask** your employer how the company proposes to assist you to keep learning throughout your career. As well as standard training sessions and programmes, there may be internal evening schools. Since you'll be investing your time, the company may be willing to cover the expense.

- **Seek out** timed project jobs, taster weeks for teams or departments, internal apprenticeships posted on notice boards or advertised within the internal job market.

- **Search on** LinkedIn, Twitter and Instagram for people with the same role as you. See what they are reading and whom they are following. Find their topics of interest and look for books, podcasts, training courses, workshops, newsgroups and internal focus groups on these topics.

- **Over** the course of the book we will introduce several ways to find out what's truly important in life. Let's start with a list of questions: How would you live your life differently, if money were no object? Where is your money spent today? What or who would you be if you knew you couldn't fail? What makes you forget to eat and sleep? Who is doing what you want to be doing?

NO ONE TOLD ME WHAT TO DO.

Dillon is often heard making this statement. Loosely translated, this means *I have absolutely zero initiative.* There are so many other things Dillon could be doing instead of sitting there, twiddling his thumbs. Dillon could ask someone what to do. He could try to find out what others in his position have done. He could brainstorm by himself or with a team member to come up with some ideas and try out a few of them.

I would like to say to Dillon: *Where is your entrepreneurial spirit? Even though your work contract doesn't say anything about being motivated, empowered and proactive, how about doing that just for the fun of it?*

Think of school or university where you sat with others long into the weekend, because you believed in it. This is an opportunity to prove yourself as someone who's not afraid to speak up, whose ideas are of value, and who is a keen creative and collaborative spirit.

WHAT TO CONSIDER OR TRY NOW

■ **Accept** that you can't change other people. Work on yourself instead. Some of the limitations of your team members stem from longstanding attitudes and patterns, the seeds of which were planted by people they had company with long before.

■ **Commit to** investing a certain amount of time and energy toward engaging your less proactive team members and inspiring them to realise their potential. You can do this even if you are not their manager. Think of yourself as a friend, an active listener, a coach. Try to understand what makes them tick. Draw out their best qualities. Start creating a personal bond by asking them about their hobbies, aspirations, dreams, and travel plans. Challenge yourself to learn something new about the person each week.[14]

- **You** can organise your conversations or considerations around a set of questions[15] that support you and others in defining what you value most for yourselves.

- **Ask** the people you are working with or leading on a project whether they truly understand why they are here. Ask them: What is your mission? What is the vision you are working towards? And what do you need from me as leader? A more dimensional approach is found in Gallup's 12 essential questions[16] on employee engagement. If you can work on these, it's a proven game-changer for productivity, sales and creativity.

- **Team** members should not compensate for such a person's lack of drive or contribution. The situation should be handled by a supervisor, who can first try to support the person by finding out where their competencies lie and assigning them to a more suitable area or task. This conversation must include clear messaging indicating a certain urgency (e.g., "Consider this a second chance").

[14] Question topics can include work, place of residence, news, and sports. See *Conversation Starters World.* "Topics to Talk About." Accessed 24 July 2020. https://bit.ly/35Z4wsm

[15] A checklist of values can help a person determine what he/she finds important, meaningful, and pertinent to one's career and life choices. See "What Are Your Values? Deciding What's Most Important in Life." Accessed 24 July 2020. https://bit.ly/3iTXPLN

[16] "The 12 Questions from the Gallup Q12 Employee Engagement Survey." Social Reacher. Accessed 24 July 2020. https://bit.ly/343GWJK

03 | **A QUESTION OF TIME**

I N CONTEMPORARY SOCIETY, THE PACE OF LIFE IS CONSTANTLY accelerating. This is evident in every aspect of our lives. The sushi you ordered will arrive in less than thirty minutes. A new iPhone model launches every year. Your Amazon package will be delivered the day after you place your order or even on the very same day. People respond to your e-mails after one hour, apologising profusely for having kept you waiting.

The world seems to spin faster and faster. It's undeniably thrilling and addictive. We race to achieve as much as we can before the close of business hours today or by the end of the quarter, at the latest. It has been a while I have seen a quarterly or annual roadmap. It would seem that most things need to be completed now, if not yesterday.

As competition mounts, companies ramp up their personnel to keep from being outpaced, deadlines get tighter, and expectation and pressure continue to grow. In every field, creation and innovation are progressing at breakneck speed. Many of the products rushed to market are designed to help us to accomplish our tasks even faster, in the hopes of saving time. And yet we seem to have less time than ever before. The days seem to be growing shorter.

Once you've raced hard enough for long enough, you meet your deadline or hit your target. Then, your reward is to forget about time—for a specified time. You dutifully set the automatic reply on your work e-mail, switch off your mobile, and go and sit on top of an Alp. *Ahhh.*

Far away from the noise and bustle, everything starts to slow down. This makes you feel strange and anxious at first. Gradually, you start to relax and feel energised. Your mind opens up. You have thoughts and insights about all kinds of things. Perched on this mountain, looking down on the little towns, you see things from a different perspective and start to connect the dots. You start to process everything that's been happening over the last few months.

When we are subjected to constant stress, our minds and bodies behave as if we are in emergency mode. We resort to using the patterns and habits we have learned, which may not always be the best or most effective response. When we are stretched to capacity, we aren't as likely to be creative or come up with fresh insights. Having time for ourselves, away from work, allows us to see the bigger picture. During some of these mountain sessions, I have reflected upon how commonly held corporate attitudes towards time often dominate the way we manage our projects and our people, often to their detriment. I'll discuss them next. There's a difference between streamlining and taking a shortcut, and it is in our best interests to understand where that distinction lies.

> 66
> Talents out there:
> Join companies
> who will invest
> in you, rather
> than you go to the
> highest bidders.

WE NEED TO HIRE MORE PEOPLE,
BUT WE DON'T HAVE TIME TO DEVELOP THEM.

Many companies operate under the impression that, while hiring people helps them to make more money, developing people doesn't generate revenue. In the long run, this simply isn't true. If you look at the world of professional football, you'll see that the best teams invest a fair amount of time and money in their training programmes. They are operating at the highest level with the best players and even they don't go straight into competition; they practice, analyse, and learn.

At any given time, there is a limited number of people available to work on a given project. We cannot simply create more employees out of nowhere. It takes time to find the right people and build high-performance teams. As Fred Brooks said, "adding people to an already late project will delay it further."[17] We tend to underestimate the effort and time it takes render people productive in a new environment. As well as the time it takes for the new hire to learn tasks and protocols and to perform these at the required pace, one has to factor in the time investment of the existing team members whose time and energy are directed toward providing training and guidance instead of producing further outputs related to the deadline.

While offshoring and nearshoring do have their charms, they also have limitations. Within the field of information technology, we are not seeing as many new initiatives in which a huge global workforce is thrown at a complex problem within a matter of weeks.

Projects grow gradually, at a healthy rate. That's exactly why we should be developing people while they work for us; though I have observed that many companies are failing to do so. As a result, their projects fall behind schedule, and their managers order overtime.

[17] Brooks, Fred. *Mythical Man Month: Essays on Software Engineering.* Addison-Wesley, 1975.

They promise this will be the last time; next time, everything will run more smoothly. In my experience, it never is, and it never does. While overtime may be a necessary compromise in certain situations, the frequency with which I have seen companies resort to this and other undesirable strategies reveals that it has become a habit.

We have all seen the movie trope of the ageing police detective who's working on his final case. After this one, he'll retire. Of course, this case is more important, pressing and complex than any of the others he has worked on, so he's forced to pull out all the stops. Just this once, he'll use unconventional methods to get the job done, because the end justifies the means. The *Lethal Weapon* movies come to mind. With every sequel, we see less conventional detective work. By the time we reach *Lethal Weapon 4*, Riggs and Murtaugh have gone completely off book. Our lives aren't like this. In the real world, Hollywood heroics won't wash. Each of us still has a long career ahead, and we should approach this with a steady rhythm of reasonable tactics. Now is the time to discard bad habits and start trying to do things better, step by step.

WHAT TO CONSIDER OR TRY NOW

- **Ensure** you are running at a sustainable pace. Ask yourself: If this project were to continue for weeks or months, could my colleagues and I still deliver it?

- **Properly** staffing projects is a crucial element. Make this a leader's job and plan this well in advance. This is a people-driven industry, and knowledge workers are hard to substitute. Directly involving teams in the process of screening applicants can yield impressive results.[18]

---

[18] Tolan, Josh. "The Most Efficient Interview Process Involves Your Whole Team." Spark Hire. Accessed 29 Aug. 2020. https://bit.ly/3cwTax3

WE DON'T HAVE TIME TO SPEND TWO DAYS ON A COURSE; DO A POWER HOUR AND SUMMARISE IT FOR THE TEAM.

I doubt that short courses designed to cover general topics for a broad range of employees provide any meaningful value. It seems to me that such programmes are formed simply so that companies can tick a box and give the impression that they're developing their staff with the minimal investment of time and money. In his book *Winning*, former General Electric chairman and CEO Jack Welch recalls that when senior managers were required to attend a five-week bootcamp, they complained that they did not have enough time to do this on top of their work in sales, marketing or product development. He goes on to reveal that none of these people were working effectively in their jobs, and that was the very reason they needed to attend the bootcamp. Numbers, sales, and customer structures had significantly changed during the time since these people had entered the workforce, and they were struggling to keep up with the times. The company was in crisis and it was getting worse every day. In fact, this measure should have been taken a long time ago.[19]

For many years, it was common practice for companies to send their employees to workshops for up to five days, on average. And yet, this was considered a burden to the organisation, in terms of the resources invested, as well as productivity lost while staff members learned to navigate new systems and techniques.

Within the last few years, the average duration decreased to two days. Even then, it has become increasingly more difficult to lure people to these training sessions. People are reluctant to turn off their phones and ignore their e-mail notifications for two days. Why do we find it so hard to focus on learning something new and

---

[19] Welch, Jack. *Winning.* Harper Business, 2005.

discussing topics with others? Why don't we consider it a privilege or a luxury to have time dedicated for this?

Presently, the average duration of a training course has dwindled to between two and six hours. Our customers often ask us to provide shortcuts to learning. They want us to present a summary of elements via a brief inspirational talk, hand out books or recommend videos. They would like us to provide material content that can be skimmed in a matter of minutes, with minimal time allocated for thought and discussion, and to digest and form an opinion about these topics. It seems that learning has been taken out of the equation. There's not enough time to analyse things from various perspectives, engage in discussion or try things out. Their attitude can be summarised in these words: *We hired you because you're an expert; just focus on your task.* As long as companies fail to coach and nurture their employees, they will not see an increase in intellectual capital.

If you want to learn how to create mind-friendly and interactive training courses, I would recommend that you explore Sharon Bowman's *Training From the back of the Room: 65 Ways to Step Aside and Let Them Learn* [20] *(TFTBOTR or TBR)* and the work of Vera Birkenbihl. The key flow of TBR is described as the 4 Cs:

1 | **Connection:** Create connections to similar things that you already know, as this will help you to retain it.

2 | **Conceptualisation:** Understand the theory and the concept we want to teach and learn.

3 | **Concrete practice:** Apply this concept in a simple practical scenario and actually put it to use once (e.g., via activity or simulation) to enforce learning.

---

[20] Bowman, Sharon. *Training from the Back of the Room: 65 Ways to Step Aside and Let Them Learn.* Pfeiffer, Dec. 2008.

4 | **Conclusion:** Consider what this means to you, how you can transfer it to your environment, what you might need, and what might hinder you.

Other key principles include the following: discussing is better than listening; moving is better than sitting; pictures are worth more than words; and making notes is better than only reading new information.

WHAT TO CONSIDER OR TRY NOW

■ **When** planning or booking your next training session, prioritise quality content instead of trying to minimise the time spent. Pay attention to how the course is delivered. Does the faculty use brain-friendly methods? Is it designed to be interactive? Does it combine theory and practical application? Are workbooks provided?

■ **When** applying for a job or meeting your new boss, be sure to ask these two questions:

1. How do you support life-long learning?

2. How is learning reflected in the company culture?

WE CAN OUTPACE THE COMPETITION BY DOING THINGS IN PARALLEL.

In our global marketplace, we see new competitors joining every day. Products have a shorter time to market (TTM). Information spreads more quickly than ever before. This competitive, hothouse atmosphere is beneficial in some ways, as it inspires everyone to keep trying harder and pushing themselves. It prevents complacency. No company can rest on its laurels, secure in the knowledge that they've done enough to keep the money flowing in. On the contrary, many companies are skittish, and rightly so.

In this climate, it is necessary to innovate, but some companies have never learned to experiment, fail spectacularly, and get up again. For them, failure is not an option. They prefer to keep doing the same things they have always done, only within a shorter span of time. In order not to be outpaced, they emphasise utilising the workforce as efficiently as possible, which they believe entails working faster and doing more things in parallel.

Outcome comes with the dedication of talent, not resource planning tools.

What does it mean to do more in parallel? People love to glorify the notion of multitasking, because, in theory, it would seem that you have gained the ability to increase your productivity to superhuman levels. Interesting tools for decreasing the amount of multitasking include Kanban and single-piece flow. Kanban is a method workflow system created by Taiichi Ohno, an industrial engineer at Toyota, to streamline manufacturing processes.[21] It takes its name from the tracking cards used in factory production. Single-piece flow (or employee-bound workflow) is a method developed in connection with Kanban.

[21] Kemp, Alex. "Taiichi Ohno: Hero of the Toyota Production System." *QAD* (blog), 15 March 2018. https://bit.ly/311EBxj

In practice, multitasking could be more accurately described as context-switching. Studies show that context-switching hinders productivity and compromises quality of work. While some jobs (e.g., co-ordination, project management, operations monitoring, incident management) require it, for brain work and conceptual work we should aim to keep context-switching to a minimum.

Multitasking is not a sign of genius, as some would have you believe; it is the nervous compulsion of a person under immense pressure. People multitask because they're trying to do too many things at once, or because they are being kept waiting by others who are too busy and are likely multitasking, too. Instead of pushing your colleague to deliver the part of the project you are awaiting, you simply switch to another task. If you spend your working life operating in this manner, you will eventually suffer from mental burnout, not to mention the frustration borne of an inability to complete anything. Continuously changing your focus from one thing to another is the primary symptom of ADHD and a secondary symptom of many other psychological conditions. I have spent a large part of this decade of my working life trying to prove to other people that context-switching is deleterious and counter-productive, in the long run.

Stop starting, start finishing work.

This brings me to a subtype of context-switching, which I like to call *Startitis*. Some people have this compulsion to start working on as many tasks as they possibly can. They are under the impression that the more tasks they start, the more productive they are. In a corporate environment, this might work for them, at least in a superficial sense. Starting lots of tasks may give your managers the feeling of significant progress.

Many managers themselves suffer from a case of startitis. They try to keep everyone busy. Partly because they don't trust people to have the initiative to get on with their projects, they want to make sure everybody has things to do and maintain a particular oversight of which elements are in the making. This is a typical old-school management technique, in which the boss has more knowledge about the tasks at hand than his employees, so he delegates small work packages to be solved piecemeal. Some would call this micro-management; Jurgen Appelo referred to it as Management 1.0 in his book *Managing for Happiness*.[22]

Furthermore, when it comes to reporting, these people can deflect questions from their bosses.

Now, let's imagine we are working on a project that is relatively new. In this case, no specific questions will be raised at the outset. Why not? So far, everything is going according to plan. It's too early to talk about delays or missed milestones. Starting the project *is* the whole project. If your boss checks in with you on an ongoing project, on which you haven't gotten very far, you can say: *We haven't done* x, y *and* z, *but exclusively work on a and b.* Or you can say: *We've started this brand new project! Everything's going according to plan.* Which of these answers do you think your boss will like more? Which would be easier for you?

These days, we have a greater range of communication tools at our disposal and can travel more conveniently and quickly than ever before. We have constant Wi-Fi connectivity. Yet we cannot think, write or speak any more quickly than our ancestors a century ago. These tools have not enhanced our ability to do things in parallel, since the bottleneck has always been us, human beings. We're knocking ourselves out trying to keep busy.

> Human evolution has plateaued. We cannot get any faster at communicating and learning.

---

[22] Appelo, Jurgen. *Management 3.0: Leading Agile Developers, Developing Agile Leaders.* Addison-Wesley Professional, 2011.

If we're doing all of this just to keep our heads above water and keep all of the proverbial plates spinning, how smart are we really? How many open topics are swimming around in your mind right now? How many issues do you still have to solve? Do you remember everything or are you constantly being reminded of something you've forgotten to do?

WHAT TO CONSIDER OR TRY NOW

- **Try to** keep context switching to a minimum or, ideally, eliminate it whenever possible. Trusted resources estimate that context switching costs you between 10 and 40 percent of your time.[23] Task switching in learned sequential procedures leads up to 300 percent overhead. [24] However, there are typical job environments where task switching belongs to the job description, e.g., in certain management positions or levels.

- **One method** of organising one's own tasks is Personal Kanban.[25] Using a Kanban system comes with the benefits of having transparency what your outstanding tasks are, limitation of your work in progress and better questioning of your strategies, e.g. your prioritisation of work.

- **To enhance** discipline and structure, practise the Pomodoro Technique,[26] a simple but fully described method to organise yourself. It includes prioritisation using a task list, time allocated for reflection and improvement, 25-minute periods of uninterrupted work time, and taking real breaks, during which you let your mind rest.

---

[23] "Multitasking: Switching Costs." American Psychological Association. 20 March 2006. https://bit.ly/34NURE2

[24] Weinstein, Yana. "The Cost of Task Switching." The Learning Scientists. Accessed 24 July 2020. https://bit.ly/2Y6EILz

[25] "Productivity 101: How to Use Personal Kanban to Visualize Your Work" *Lifehacker* (website). Accessed 16 June 2020. https://bit.ly/32TP7Yq

[26] "The Pomodoro Technique: Do More and Have Fun with Time Management." Franceso Cirillo (website). Accessed 24 July 2020. https://bit.ly/30WS4q6

DON'T ASK ME WHY I'M HERE. I HAVE ABSOLUTELY NO DOMAIN OR TECHNICAL KNOWLEDGE ABOUT THIS TOPIC.

It's time to meet Carey. She's focused, sharp, and highly motivated, but her ambition is completely self-serving. She's driven by the desire to further her own career and status. Carey actually made the above statement to me. If I hadn't heard it with my own ears, I wouldn't have believed it. *What a weird flex,* I thought. *Is it just a bad joke? Is she trying to be self-deprecating?* I was baffled.

Carey Career-Driven - nowhere and everywhere.
A few flaws which are bad for the company, but productive for her. Call her the "successful project person".

Imagine my surprise when I discovered that over the years Carey has been involved in several projects of varying degrees of success—ranging from mediocre to superb. She's always hopping from one project to the next. Although Carey doesn't necessarily bring value to the team, she has an overinflated sense of her skills and achievements and has drilled this into everyone around her. She can be rather aggressive and has a tendency to browbeat others and force her opinions upon them. Carey wants to make herself heard, not because she wants to contribute anything, but because she wants to make her presence known. This is a distraction technique. By always making sure that everyone knows she's present and available, she deflects responsibility and accountability. People feel too intimidated to question her. This works well for Carey, in terms of getting people to leave her alone, but it is not terribly helpful for the success of the project.

The question remains: *What motivates people like Carey to stay on this project, even when they can't truly contribute?* She's creating overhead and constraints on the rest of the project, since she often creates issues that need to be cleaned up by others. Even worse, other project members may behave as she does. Efficiency and productivity fly out the window.

WHAT TO CONSIDER OR TRY NOW

- **Value** and embrace diversity. We tend to favour people who think and behave as we do. This is problematic, in that it prevents leaders from hiring or staffing a diverse mix of people on projects. Try to become more aware of your own biases.[27] Democratising decisions (e.g., making hiring decisions as a group) can help guard against your personal biases.

- **To learn** more about the cognitive biases that affect our decisions, check out this comprehensive infographics "Every Single Cognitive Bias"[28] (way beyond 150 biases categorized) or this more explanatory Infographic[29] (list of crucial 50 biases).

- **Learn** about what makes different kinds of people tick. Try to see the good qualities in each individual and figure out how to build upon these qualities and put them to use. Rather than trying to change people, try to match them with the task and environment that will help them to flourish.

- **You** can draw the best out of people if you understand how to get along with different characters. You may find it helpful to learn about various systems for assessing personality types, including the Myers-Briggs Type Indicator (MBTI), the DiSC assessment, Merrill and Reid's social styles model, and the 16Personalities.com[30] test. However, a personality type can get overruled or redefined by group dynamics.

---

[27] Dwyer, Christopher. "12 Common Biases that Affect How We Make Everyday Decisions." 7 Sept. 2018. Psychology Today. https://bit.ly/32PNqeg

[28] Desjardins, Jess. "Every Single Cognitive Bias in One Infographic." Visual Capitalist. 25 Sept. 2017 https://bit.ly/2RMQ3HJ

[29] Lu, Marcus. "50 Cognitive Biases in the Modern World." Visual Capitalist. 1 Feb. 2020. https://bit.ly/3iTJPla

[30] You can take the DISC and MBTI tests at truity.com, and the 16 personalities test at https://www.16personalities.com/

YOU CAN NEVER HAVE TOO MANY WORKS IN PROGRESS.

As we've already discussed, Kanban can be applied to any process primarily to optimize throughout. Kanban can be used at the individual or team level, and even at higher levels of scaled and enterprise (as explained in this article[31] by Klaus Leopold). Kanban is mostly connected to the visible parts in form of Kanban boards. The work-in-progress (WIP) limits restrict the number of tasks you may have open at any time in each stage (or board column) of the workflow.[32] This is supposed to prevent bottlenecks and overloads by ensuring that you start new tasks only once you have made sufficient progress with other tasks. This makes sense, particularly when working with a team. When you are stuck with something, instead of starting something new, you would try to solve another task that is still in progress. Ideally, your work-in-progress limit should be *one*, and the sooner you come to understand this, the better. You will likely be tempted to exceed this limit; however, I don't advise raising it, as this would defeat the purpose of having it at all.

One of the dangers of having too many WIPs at any given time is the incessant demand for progress reports. Each time we take on a new project, we invite into our lives a number of individuals who will habitually request instant messages, e-mail, telephone or in-person updates. This constant pressure to answer them creates a huge drain on our time and makes us feel overloaded and overwhelmed. We are too busy writing and speaking to them to actually work on the project itself.

---

[31] Leopold, Klaus. "Flight Levels: The Organizational Improvement Levels." LEANability. 29 April 2017. [Blog] https://bit.ly/33SG3IN

[32] "Kanban." Agile Alliance (website). Accessed 16 June 2020. https://www.agilealliance.org/glossary/kanban/.

Having too many tasks open at once creates cognitive dissonance; whatever we are doing, we have the sense that that we should be working on something else, as well as reporting to everyone whose projects we are working on, and those whose projects we are too busy to work on. We shift into survival mode, simply trying to clear our plates and rush to the next item. With this chaotic mindset, creativity and passion go straight out the window. We struggle to get anything done at all, not to mention producing work of the highest quality.

WHAT TO CONSIDER OR TRY NOW

- **Slow down.** Lothar Seiwert, a German author and speaker on time management and life leadership, says: "If you are in a hurry, go slowly." I would suggest that you also take regular breaks for rest and reflection.

- **Whenever** you feel your thoughts starting to spin, get them out of your mind by writing them down. David Allen, the inventor of the Getting Things Done (GTD) Methodology suggests using one trusted system[33] to do so. Having multiple lists, tools, and apps can create even more stress and disorder in the long run.

- **Start** incorporating the six core practices that make up the methodology of Kanban:

  1. Visualise your work, which should lead to higher transparency for all involved persons

  2. Limit work in progress (WIP), which should lead to higher throughput

---

[33] Talbert, Robert. "GTD for Academics: Simple Trusted System." Robert Talbert (personal website). 10 March 2017. https://bit.ly/32WPaml

3. Make policies explicit, which should lead to consistent, defined and efficient flow

4. Manage flow, which should focus you in accordance to the design of the board and the underlying process towards achieving flow of the items on the board

5. Implement feedback loops, which should help you to learn, optimise and improve the flow and products built

6. Improve collaboratively and evolve experimentally, which should inspire everyone involved in the process to invest in incremental improvements co-created and inspired by all.

WE USE TIME-BUFFERS AS SAFETY NETS - THE WIDER THE MARGIN, THE BETTER!

As Murphy's law dictates: "If anything can go wrong, it will." Projects get more and more complex as political, technical and human influences impact risks and assumptions about resource usage. The traditional solution is to add safety time or buffers to tasks to allow for schedule slippage and unplanned events.

This attitude is thoroughly wrongheaded. Using buffers will not magically enable teams to meet impossibly tight deadlines. Once employees realise that they are being routinely pushed to the limit, they will simply build even more buffers into their calculations to get some breathing space. When asked how long a particular task will take, employees will automatically add a buffer of x percent. This tactic is exploited by employees just as resource planning is exploited by companies. A lot of energy becomes redirected into politics, and this erodes the collaborative spirit that engenders good product creation.

WHAT TO CONSIDER OR TRY NOW

- **If you** frequently experience the just described dynamic, this may be a sign that you are working in an environment that fails to provide employees with psychological safety. Unhealthy work cultures are typified by a lack of openness and transparency, and a sense that employees are forced into dishonest and duplicitous behaviour. If you push people and you don't listen to them, the simple mechanisms of project management won't get you anywhere.

- **Go through** the following list to help you ascertain whether your work environment is toxic and seek to address any issues from this list that you recognise:

  - ☑ When a decision is reached, you are challenged shortly afterwards by the very same people who participated in making that decision.

  - ☑ A sizable portion of employees suffer from imposter syndrome.

  - ☑ When you raise concerns in a one-to-one conversation, the relevant person fails to follow through on offering feedback to peers or management.

  - ☑ It's impossible to take a break. Employees are encouraged to work overtime and to go without holiday time.

  - ☑ When people make mistakes, they seem to be unable to forgive themselves and move on.

  - ☑ Even when management makes efforts that appear to have positive underlying intent, employees suspect them of having malignant intent.

- **Take** control by reading on the Critical Chain Method[34] which will help you understand time buffers and deliver a high quality of project management.

---

[34] Reddy, Sudarsan. "Critical Chain Project Management Methodology and Buffers Explained." *Medium*. 27 Feb. 2019. https://bit.ly/3kCwTjT

WE DON'T PLAN WORK, INSTEAD WE DO RESOURCE PLANNING ON OUR PEOPLE.

In the 1950s, while working in the field of motivation theory based on Abraham Maslow's hierarchy of needs, the psychologist Douglas McGregor observed that most management styles are informed by one of two distinctive attitudes, which he labelled Theory X and Theory Y. Theory X assumes that the average employee lacks ambition, and prefers to avoid responsibility and pursue individual goals; while Theory Y assumes that the typical employee is intrinsically motivated and, within the right environment, enjoys working and feels personally rewarded by working.[35] These theories delineate the polar extremes of the spectrum rather than representing commonly held notions.

Many companies today still operate under management styles that lean towards Theory X. In such environments, resource management is considered a viable coordination mechanism for parallel work. This strategy is based on the presumption that employees won't do anything unless they're assigned specific tasks. They treat people as resources, because resources are easier to manage. So, they fire up their resource-management planning tool and that's where it all starts to go downhill. All too often, I see that companies don't plan how they'll do the work as much as they plan how they'll use their people.

> If you treat people as if they are resources, you will lose their respect.

There is an expectation for employees to meet every demand. Everything that is requested must be accomplished, no matter what. We pay our project managers to come up with a sophisticated plan, hoping to ensure that our available resources will be used as efficiently as possible, so that we'll get everything done. In hindsight, there is always room for improvement. It appears that we could have achieved more, if only we had worked more efficiently.

---

[35] Morse, John J. and Jay W. Lorsch. "Beyond Theory Y." *Harvard Business Review* (website). From the May 1970 issue. https://hbr.org/1970/05/beyond-theory-y

WHAT TO CONSIDER OR TRY NOW

- **Work** with your team or with specific individuals to get an honest estimate. Guide them or use open-ended constructive questions to show them how to improve their estimations skills. After completion of the estimated work, take time to reflect by comparing the initial estimate with the result. Was there anything that could have been foreseen? Were the delays due to volatility, uncertainty, complexity and ambiguity (also referred to as VUCA)? Adjust your estimation model, if possible.

- **Use** lean techniques to improve your plans and make time-frames more realistic. These would include:

  - ☑ Instead of planning periods of one year or six months, plan for shorter timeframes as by the quarter, month or fortnight. Shorter projects have a much higher possibility of finishing on time and within budget (Use this source[36] for an overview on statistics supporting this).

  - ☑ Use an optimised structure organised by the flow of work from the customer (e.g., order) back to the customer (e.g., delivery of goods). By avoiding function-oriented organisation, you can minimise handovers between functions, thus reducing the risk of error and the loss of time and effort incurred by siloed resource management. Siloed management layers often cause delays, as they require more management, reporting and decision meetings, which may delay progress, and, from a content perspective, don't lead to better decisions. Ideal team settings occur in small setups with Feature[37] or Scrum Teams. Each team is staffed by all skills needed to fulfil its mission and an overall leadership is appointed.

[36] Tavrizyan, Karine. "16 Project Management Stats You Can't Ignore." *Medium*. 11 Feb. 2019. https://bit.ly/2RQnWHo

[37] "Feature Teams." Feature Teams. Accessed 29 Aug. 2020 https://featureteams.org/

I AM DOING THREE JOBS IN PARALLEL; NO ONE ELSE IS CAPABLE OF TAKING OVER MY ROLE.

In every company, you will find at least one individual whose superpower is to occupy some unique and complex constellation of roles, which renders them—according to them, at least—indispensable. Let's call this person Susanne.

Susanne Superhero - very skilled. All can do. When you need to get something done, she will solve it. Very often sadly also a lonely wolf.

Susanne, the superhero, is well established within the company, having honed her skills through various projects and formed a perfect network of colleagues. She is fully aware of her unique position, but she isn't arrogant about it. She is needed, and she knows this. Susanne has a few shortcomings (namely communication, sharing and teamwork), but nobody is too concerned about them since she is so instrumental to securing project success.

No project can survive without Susanne. While her colleagues may view her superhero status as a quirky and admirable trait, to any outsider the precarity of this situation is patently obvious. If Susanne takes leave, due to illness or burnout, or if she exits the company, it will create a bottleneck and the project will be delayed until someone else is hired and acquires the training and experience to replace her, which takes at least months, don't be fooled here.

In many cases, this situation serves, whether consciously or unconsciously, to protect Susanne's job security. Whenever the company attempts to orchestrate a handover or delegation of these tasks by asking her to train others to perform some of these duties, Susanne cannot cope with the threat to her dominance. As any attempt to sabotage such efforts by causing a bottleneck or ensuring that the quality of work declines will reflect badly upon her, she will likely concede to the new initiative but only up to a certain point. Susanne may withhold vital information or put up roadblocks to protect her expert status. If the new trainees manage to succeed in learning the ropes anyway, they will usurp Susanne's source of power. Perhaps this is why (like most superheroes) Susanne prefers to work alone.

I have met so many Susannes at so many different organisations. It's always the same old story. You have to beg them to share their knowledge. They make you feel dumb for asking, as if you should already know, and they dole it out piecemeal, if at all. It's like drawing blood from a stone. They claim they're too busy to work as part of the team.

Because working collaboratively won't bring Susanne the glory she seeks, she would rather sit back and watch other people flail so she can jump in at the last moment and save the day. Susanne prefers to remain the lone wolf and maintain her particular brand of mystique.

Some of the reasons why superheroes like Susanne are a weak link in any organisation:

- One person cannot be scaled up for larger projects and tasks
- Lowers the truck factor[38] This refers to how many or what percentage of your team members can be hit by a truck before you would be in serious trouble. See: 38
- Not sustainable
- Even routine absences create friction and bottlenecks
- Not a team player
- Suboptimal decision making

[38] Bowler, Michael. *Truck Factor*. 15 May 2005. https://bit.l/31VYcOp

Slowly and surely, she is edging herself out of the loop. She will struggle to remain current with the latest features and trends. With every advance of the abstraction level in technology, she will become less crucial. It will likely be a matter of years before this becomes apparent to her and the company who employs her. Unless Susanne changes her ways, she will eventually face the consequences.

WHAT TO CONSIDER OR TRY NOW

- **If your** work environment has a superhero culture,[39] you can start taking the following steps to address this problem:

  - ☑ Stop glorifying and rewarding unhealthy attitudes and relationships to work and reinforce healthy ones

  - ☑ Coach the heroes to take a healthier approach to work

  - ☑ Together as a team, start to redefine healthy work values

  - ☑ Introduce discipline and structure, and install some processes to streamline and force heroes into a healthier working mode

  - ☑ Discuss the topic and reflect upon the risks

  - ☑ Management must be clear that this behaviour of siloed and egotistical over-performing is just as detrimental to the organisation as underperforming.

---

[39] Blank, Steve. "Hacking a Corporate Culture: Stories, Heroes, and Rituals in Startups and Companies." 9 September 2015. https://bit.ly/2DYHS7N

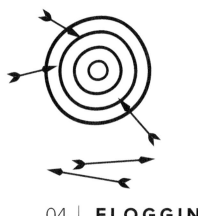

04 | **FLOGGING
A DEAD HORSE**

Now, let's go back to Carlo and the story we began in **Chapter 1 We are all customers.** We'll begin by rewinding four years to when this project began. At this time, I wasn't yet involved with the project, so I will share all of the relevant facts that were shared with me.

WE'LL STICK TO THE TIMETABLE, NO MATTER WHAT

The project leaders chose a technology, fixed a project finishing date, and agreed upon a desired set of functionalities—everything the old software was able to do, and more. People got to work. After some time, it came to light that various steps of this process were being established differently throughout the country, as the set of the unique IT-product wasn't able to cover all of these working styles. Therefore, people were appointed to travel around the country conducting a thorough analysis of the various working styles that had surfaced and how these challenges were being tackled. So far, so good. Keep in mind, none of this was planned at the outset. The timetable went out the window.

It also became necessary to find a way for people on the project to work together. Their assigned task was to renew the different forms of software applications and integrate them all into one application that would help provide a better and faster service to Carlo and countless others like him. Now, they had to do analysis, interviews, and interpret certain behaviours, and they had to understand the old set of applications and transfer this to state-of-the-art software supposed to work now on tablets and mobiles which had emerged in the meantime. A common operating model was to plan, build, verify, and roll it out. It was supposed to be very straightforward, without any (or many) problems allowed. They would have just one shot, and it had to work. If it failed, they would fall behind the timeline. Every time an issue emerged that they had not anticipated, they would fall further behind the timeline. Every change request that was raised along the way affected their timeline. To make things worse, people would be dissatisfied with what they saw, unless they had been included along the way. But it wasn't that easy to keep them updated, since they didn't want to see incremental changes and improvements; they wanted to see a final design and functionality.

Never compromise on quality to save time.

Time, or the lack of it, is the common factor for an optimisation which leads eventually to bad quality. Naturally, the internal stakeholders had an interest in delivering the project in time and on budget. Imagine, after waiting for a very long time to see results, receiving a solution that falls short of your expectations.

At this point, Carlo had yet to witness any improvement. Until the new application got the green light and was rolled out in production, Carlo was still dealing with the struggling customer service agents. Let's just hope Carlo was dealing with the same agent throughout his process (which may have taken a few days, weeks or months) and that this agent had learned how to navigate the old set of applications in the meantime.

Additional pressure stemmed from the fact that the current set of applications was simultaneously undergoing development. Therefore, even if Carlo's customer service agent understood everything well, the current set of applications would inevitably be subject to changes. If Carlo were to search for another job at any time within the next two years, he would be forced to repeat much of the process he had already endured.

So, they had an initial timeline, including the scope of work and delivery date. In parallel, it emerged that a vast amount of unforeseen analysis had to be carried out within the company's central organisation and at various service centres across the country. Along the way, the decision was taken not to decommission the other applications, even though the initial idea was to build more and more functionality into the newly created application. Therefore, new features also had to be developed within the other applications. Internal competition emerged between the teams who were working to the reach of usage of its IT products. They were responsible for the applications and they all wanted to hold onto their jobs, whether they were external consultants, who wished to protect their positions and the safety of the project, or internal colleagues, who are equally as averse to an uncertain future.

The newly appointed teams had neither any knowledge about their team members (who they had never worked with) nor any domain know-how. Domain know-how is knowledge about an organisation's internal processes, including understanding the power structures and knowing which people to contact to get proper answers to one's questions. To succeed within a company setup, one must have an understanding of the internally used abbreviations, software architecture, and relationships between teams and departments.

The new teams had to acquire all of this knowledge while keeping up with the changing requirements and an ever-shifting application landscape. Furthermore, as they were using technology that would soon be rendered obsolete, they also had to work to maintain their IT-architecture standards without losing relevance. They had to negotiate all of the above while working on what had initially been set up as a fixed-time, fixed-scope project for a relatively uncomplicated application. Or so they had been told.

This is yet another recurring theme. I have seen it time and time again. At some point, we always come to realise that all of this could have been foreseen from the very beginning, had we not been so naïve.

WHAT TO CONSIDER OR TRY NOW

■ **In today's** complex and rapidly changing world, the scope of a project is always changing as well, which makes it difficult for teams to predict milestones and release dates. While there is no way to guarantee delivery in time and on budget, applying the steps outlined below will help you and your team to come closer to meeting your shared goals.

☑ Acknowledge that there will be changes and allow for these in your planning but be transparent with buffers and contingencies. Communicate when and how these may be used, and for what purpose. When utilised, ensure they are properly prioritised and that you get the best support to use the allocated budget wisely and in a way that would meet the approval of your sponsors.

☑ Perform a thorough risk analysis. Involve stakeholders, sponsors, all parties directly involved with the product as users, and your functional and technical support and sales and marketing teams.

☑ Evaluate your product and its handling and processes with the end users. Conduct a simulation or evaluate it via paper prototype and a step-by-step walkthrough with all involved persons.

☑ Be honest with yourself and your team members throughout the process.

☑ Openly address impediments and changes to get support and create awareness.

☑ Keep focus on the team as a whole, as well as keeping tabs on individual persons. Even when it's feasible to complete all tasks within the estimated time frame, parallel work skews your estimates by adding time for task switching.

■ **Plan** for change management. As well as changing the company's processes and its organisational culture; every new product or service entails change for the people involved. From the first day of the project onward, you will need to carry out change management activities, including conducting stakeholder analysis, assessing and meeting communication and involvement requirements, and providing the necessary guidance and training sessions.

■ **Adding** or creating new teams involves much more than simply finding a number of skilled people and calling them a team. When creating new teams or adding people to a project, consider the following practices.

☑ Establish a clear onboarding process to get people up to speed with the required knowledge. Invite newcomers to communities of practice to learn tools and methods. Providing knowledge transfer sessions via video or audio recordings is the most efficient way to conduct such recurring training. In a tutorial session, walk them through the steps they should later execute by themselves. Provide them with a handbook outlining key routines and a list or a source of best practice sample cases.

☑ Integrate new teams or people into the existing team and VIP structure. You might consider conducting a culture-appropriate team building session to get everyone acquainted. This should be interactive and playful and include various levels and perspectives. For a hands-on quick start, assign more experienced individuals to work with newcomers (also known as pairing). Introduce the important subject matter experts or central governance for their areas. You can do this in person or provide an accessible overview (such as a who's who).

☑ Keep in mind that there will be a learning curve. Allow some extra time in your calculations when making plans and forecasts for teams that include newcomers.

AS LONG AS THERE IS FUNDING, WE'LL KEEP GOING

Three years into the project, no major breakthroughs had yet been achieved. It was time to try something new or to stop the project altogether. The decision was taken to learn from past experiences and improve.

The effort required to keep up with the everchanging requirements had led the teams to miss many milestones. It wasn't as if they had achieved nothing at all—they had succeeded in producing software and building functionality. Pilot areas, including entire departments, were working with the new application. Millions of euros had been invested in this project and many people had spent countless hours working towards its successful outcome. Eventually, it surfaced that the technology utilised by this application was out of date and had been chosen simply because it was required by company policy (which we later found out had not been updated in the last four years before project start).

Preconceived notions are the nemeses of putting a plan into practice. To put it simply, the more you presume from the very beginning, the less you try to change these preconceptions later on. And whether these are based on experience or bias, whether they have been proven or one simply chose a stance and stuck to it, such assumptions increasingly become the norm and are taken for granted. I have seen this situation playing out too many times to count. People tend to make rules based on their preconceptions and biases, and very early on these become engraved in stone. It seems that one is powerless to change them, even after the assumptions on which they are based have proven to be false, and even when it is obvious almost from the outset that one should have taken a different direction or, at least certain different steps.

At this point, it was clearly necessary to change course or abandon ship. Naturally, discontinuing the project was out of the ques tion. This was largely due to the fear of losing face. Leaders wanted to protect their reputations; entire teams had been hired, and the companies who'd brokered those deals didn't want to suggest stopping this project for fear of being held liable.

The decision was taken to change captains, and a new project manager was appointed. Most of the teams were to keep building the application, since they had spent the last three years acquiring all of the requisite domain know-how and technological savvy. The new project manager was a tough guy. Everyone believed in his ability to steer the project, keep everyone in check, and stick to the timeline. A second in charge was appointed to handle all the internal stakeholders and departments, so as to make this project the focal point and de facto new standard for all upcoming software developments. One crucial thing was missing: a proposed approach to developing the software. An Agile approach proved best suited to the incremental release of results. Never mind that the application had since been rendered obsolete, as the technology with which it had been built was now out of service, and the analyses had revealed that the various processes being used across the country could not be built into a single application—having a new project manager and operating model would solve everything. I have observed this pattern enacted in so many projects. The fundamental issue lies in the sequence of decisions typically leading up to a change of direction that very often ends in using an Agile approach. If you've had similar experiences in the past, you will be familiar with the mixture of anger and bitterness I felt when I was asked to join the project and heard all of this. I was ready to throw my laptop out of the window and then run over it with a car. At this point, it was already too late. This ship already had too many holes and had sustained too much damage.

WHAT TO CONSIDER OR TRY NOW

- **This** story demonstrates what is likely to happen when there is a lack of transparency and openness in an organisation's culture. We need to strive to create a culture of mistakes. While this term is often misinterpreted to mean a culture that engenders mistakes, it actually refers to a culture that appropriately responds to and learns from its mistakes. We should understand that true progress and innovation incur a high chance of failure, and that making mistakes is a necessary step in the learning process, and therefore it is not appropriate to punish people for failing or to lay blame. We should be striving to create a culture of appropriate risk-taking to solve problems, achieve goals and overcome obstacles.

- **When** starting new projects, you may want to make the distinction between fixed and variable solution intent. Consider what is fixed for you and what might or should be questioned or challenged. Even fixed conditions may need to be checked if the questions come from a reliable and proven source. However, even in such cases, there is no way to re-do everything mostly due to time or budget restrictions.

- **Changing** your project management method is, in itself, unlikely to render a doomed project successful. Even though Agile methods are the most appropriate manner in which to manage initiatives, they are no silver bullet. To learn more about how to choose the most appropriate method for your project and to properly execute it, we recommend getting familiar with the WHOW matrix,[40] the Stacey matrix,[41] or the Cynefin framework.[42]

[40] "Stacey Matrix." Praxis. Accessed 22 Sept. 2020. https://bit.ly/2FTaDnb

[41] "WHOW Matrix." Praxis. Accessed 22 Sept. 2020. https://bit.ly/3cjzNHD

[42] "Cynefin framework." Wikipedia. Last modified 2 Sept. 2020. https://bit.ly/3mKoGMH

CHANGING OUR APPROACH WILL CHANGE EVERYTHING

Despite our better judgement, we kept on trying to achieve the impossible. In the aftermath (or Phase Two, as it was referred to, since this sounds more positive and planned) the strategy was to shoot at the same objective with a different weapon. *Hey, we used a slingshot before, so now let's try it with a peashooter! By the way, our target is a fighter jet.*

Phase Two commenced with the formation of Agile teams. Many established practices were kept in place. During this time, two issues came up that were particularly striking. The first issue was that the company altered the way it managed projects and handled its staff without properly communicating to its employees the reasoning and purpose behind the implemented changes, and this resulted in widespread paranoia and misunderstanding.

Prior to this, the company's stance had been to command and control, taking a very strong top-down approach and withholding information from the majority of its employees for as long as possible. All of a sudden, management completely overhauled the company's culture, mindset and way of working. The idea was to push for change. People who had formerly been sequestered were singled out to speak up and raise concerns. The teams, newly formed, were expected to interact in a completely different manner, disregarding the way they had worked together in the past.

There's a fine line between what's necessary and what constitutes a last-ditch attempt at redemption.

Naturally, many people thought that their performance had fallen short and that they were now being given one last chance to prove themselves. Tensions ran high, and everyone wondered what had gone wrong. Large numbers of valued employees left the company under the impression that their competences were no longer deemed necessary, since they were now being addressed via their teams instead of receiving direct communication. Many of these were external employees who were not directly employed by this company, and, having spent so many years on the project, they sought out other opportunities.

The second issue was a systemic failure that came to light when the new teams were formed. In the first few weeks, almost nothing was accomplished apart from attempting to build trust and modes of collaboration. Everything else stalled out during this time. There was no fluent change from one situation to the next, and no intermediate steps were taken. Within the newly formed structure, the value creation teams were supported by satellite teams, who monitored the whole and provided help wherever it was needed (usually in specialised areas, as satellites offer specific solutions. These teams lay the groundwork for all standards and provided the technological basis and integration into the rest of the organisation).

Several of these satellite teams, each of which had been staffed by a single external company, had formed their team hierarchies and career arcs over the course of the three years they'd spent working together on the first phase of the project. It wasn't possible to break up these teams, as would have been necessary, because some very strong key players had already earned trust within the organisation. Therefore, no one considered these teams to be bottlenecks or innovation-blockers.

A few months later, a discussion arose around their value-add to the whole project. Eventually, the absurdity of this area of the project came to light. One exchange, which we took as asymptomatic and indicative of failure, went as follows:

We asked: *Was the task on which you were working aligned with the other teams' tasks, and what value did it bring to the project?*

The team replied: *We assumed that what we were doing would help the other teams, even though we never specifically asked them, since we had so much to do. We just thought, let's work on this thing and, in a few months, we will show them. Plus, what we did had been aligned with the rest of the organisation and will be rolled out with other projects as well. Much of our time goes into the development of features necessary for other projects. If it weren't for the company's other projects, which were to make use of these developments—if they didn't exist, this project would gain the benefits even earlier. But anyway, we did not believe it would be needed earlier.*

Isn't that weird? All along, the members of the satellite teams were sitting right next to the teams who were working on the rest of their project. The project had rented the whole space with the express purpose of allowing the teams to work in close proximity. They were no more than a few meters away from each other. Yet the satellite teams never found the time to go over and communicate with the other teams. They hardly knew any of the names of the other teams' members. I get agitated every time I think back to this encounter. The teams were sitting within earshot of each other.

Strategically, they placed more value on serving the rest of the organisation, and its many projects, than on this, their original main and exclusive project. They prioritised strategy and long-term value above all else, instead of aligning with the other teams and striving for value creation and delivery, only to come up with something which might or might not fit everyone.

With all of the aforementioned challenges, it seemed unlikely we would hit our target. But we did our best to adapt to the situation, to make the impossible happen, and to create something beautiful and useful.

We were chasing ghosts, and we knew it. Pressure was coming from all sides. The numbers were against us, but we couldn't convince anyone. Besides, no one wanted to be the bearer of bad news. A tendency had emerged—a form of weakness I have encountered all too often and which we will see enacted many times—of passing the buck. No one wants to take the initiative, as doing so would require them to talk about uncomfortable topics, such as failure, and the inability to meet targets.

At a certain point, we gathered all the historical data we could find, conducted an empirical analysis, and applied estimations to the work in our backlog. This took a considerable amount of time. As the project was ever growing in scope, it was hard for us to know how much work was still required at any given time. Examining the details and making ballpark estimations helped us to calculate best-case and worst-case scenarios. This was communicated on a weekly basis, and it got worse from week to week. We were forced to question how the project's progress had been measured prior to this, if not simply by counting work packages.

Let's say we are setting up a moving company. Every time we need to move the contents of one flat to another flat, we need to calculate how long it will take to pack everything up and put it into a van. The quick-draw answer is: *It depends.*

In fact, it is rather simple. Many items can be packed into boxes of a standard size. In addition, we have large, bulky items, including lamps, kitchen and other household appliances, bed frames, mattresses, cupboards, and so on. However, if we have prior moving experience, we can make an educated guess. The more moving jobs we carry out, the more experience we'll gain, and the more accurate our estimates will be.

If it is our first job, then counting the pieces is the easiest way to measure how long it will take to move the items from one flat to another. The same applies when developing software. We'd break the work down into measurable, tangible components or packages. For the sake of simplicity, let's call them items. Then we'd measure the number of items. It's a start—before you know anything, you can do that. You know approximately a hundred items need to be done to finish the project. Start tracking as much as you can, and you will be able to make a ballpark estimate of when you will be done with the hundred items. This project didn't have any such system in place. Instead, it used more complicated yet precise methods of measuring, all of which failed to give us any answer at all.

We decided to hijack one of the weekly status meetings so that we could exclusively share the scenario analysis depicting real data up to that point and projections of best-case, standard, and worst-case scenarios.

It may seem odd that we had to hijack the weekly status meeting to be able to discuss the status of the project. Surely the purpose of the weekly status meeting is to address the most important issues and concerns. Ideally, that would be the case, but the teams were still labouring under the delusion that is was possible to fix the plan and steer the project towards success without asking existential risk questions about it. But now the writing was on the wall. The best-case scenario was that we would miss our delivery date by two years and six months.

> All too often, status meetings focus solely on escalations, blaming others and abdicating responsibility.

We put in milestones and year markers. Up until this point, this had never been done. Over the following weeks, as the numbers were checked and re-checked, it became evident to everyone that we had reached the tipping point. The project had to be stopped, as there was no way of getting it back on track.

By this time, eighty million euros had been spent on developing this application, yet only a few departments were using it. Getting the project to the stage where its results would be accepted by users would require a minimum further investment of fifty million euros, if there wasn't any more increase in scope. It would cost even more if the scope were to increase, which was more than likely.

After some discussion, we were delegated to inform people of the current situation. The project was discontinued, but because everything had to be documented, it took four weeks to close it down. During this time, the core team members (comprising nearly a third of the entire workforce) continued doing knowledge transfer. The company's intention was to keep its intellectual property inhouse and transfer the knowledge to the next project. All other areas had their applications still in use. Some of them had reached an astonishingly mature realisation of processing and efficiency in helping the customer service agents to do their jobs.

This would have helped applicants like Carlo to more quickly acquire a new job. Sadly, the company has never fulfilled its objective of providing a better service with this particular project.

Why not bury something that had already been declared dead? In all honesty, it had died two years earlier, long before we started the second phase.. Admitting defeat a bit sooner would have spared Carlo some time and frustration and saved the company a lot of money.

> Avoiding politics is never easy. With data, the facts are hard to argue.

What can we learn from this story? While you cannot control the external factors, you can commit to a particular code of conduct. In the case study above, combining a certain standard of ethics and behaviour with talent—honesty, initiative-taking, professionalism, intuition, and creativity, in particular—would have helped the team to mitigate or even resolve the problems they encountered along the way.

WHAT TO CONSIDER OR TRY NOW

- **As** we've already mentioned, any change of methods, practices or processes requires the people involved to change as well. We have observed that it is not enough to change their behavioural patterns; it is necessary to address the principles or beliefs underlying these patterns as well. When implementing Agile methods, you will likely encounter such situations. For example, when changing the modus of intra-team collaboration, you may touch on general or company-specific elements of the culture. Say you have a company in which the culture has always been one of command and control, and all of a sudden, individuals are expected to take the initiative to self-organise. Even if this is something they have always wanted to do, you cannot expect that they will know how to approach it. As this was never previously required, nor was it permitted, there needs to be a learning path. It is always risky with no guarantee for the expected results to introduce any behavioural changes, no matter how simple or instinctual these may appear to be. Particularly in an environment where the organisational culture is deeply ingrained, and where employees are suddenly required to make a change that is completely at odds with the previously established culture, it is crucial to provide them with the proper training, guidance and support.

- **We** often hear it said that the world we are living in is volatile, uncertain, complex and ambiguous (VUCA). Systems thinking is a knowledge area that aims to support actions and decisions in such an environment. For example, as it tells us that the complexity of a system derives not from the number of its elements but from the number of connections between those elements, we know that any complexity arising within a team does not derive from the sheer number of people involved and it is necessary to take a closer look at the connections between those people.

cross-functional or feature team. By this we mean a stable, long-lived, empowered group formed of between five and nine people who have the same mission and vision and, between them, have all the requisite skills to carry this mission all the way from the person who identifies the need to the one who consumes the product. The cohesion of such teams give them the ability to streamline communication and handovers, which makes them fast. Teams containing all the functions needed to build a product solution are able to deliver more consistent and innovative solutions than teams split up according to specific functions (e.g., analysis, building, testing).

- **If you** are interested in learning participative, quick and rough estimation methods for high volumes of items, we recommend learning about affinity estimation[43] or magic estimation.[44] Both of these methods involve estimating elements in relation to each other, forming buckets of similarly sized elements, and calculating the whole effort by interpolating from any known quantity within these buckets. This can stem from a similarity to an already completed item or other historical data.

[43] "Affinity Estimating: A HOW-TO" GettingAgile. Accessed 11 Oct. 2020.
https://bit.ly/2GRj16W

[44] "Magic Estimation Game: How to Do It Remotely" Inovex. Accessed 11 Oct. 2020.
https://bit.ly/3lBJxAc

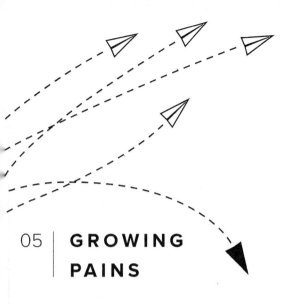

05 | **GROWING PAINS**

REAL CHANGE INVOLVES TRANSFORMATION. SOME COMPANIES are made uneasy by the idea of transformation, as it suggests a radical shift from one form to another. They would prefer to call their transformations *initiatives*. Or, they talk about evolutionary change. *We're evolving.*

Pardon me for laughing. Change is change, no matter what you call it. And yes, it is painful for everyone involved. You can dress it up to make it sound fancy or dress it down to make it less intimidating, but no matter what you call it, you have to accept the fact that you are going to change something. Small shifts will accumulate over time to create something new. Even evolutionary change will lead inexorably to a radical metamorphosis eventually.

> Change is a delicate topic, and delicate topics should be approached delicately.

I recently listened to the *Pessimists Archive*, a hilarious podcast about the history of change, and specifically, about why people tend to reject change. It became clear that it is never about the change itself. The speaker brings up all kinds of examples, including scooters, medicine, and seatbelts. He argues that people have always feared being told what to do and how to do it.[45]

We need to learn to question our resistance to change. It's time to adopt a growth mindset, where you understand the options you have. You need to have a guiding star, a vision, something you truly desire. Something you burn for. Something which gives you meaning and purpose. This is how you entrust an organisation, a department or a team with prescribed movements that are fully supported, and which may or may not work. Consider this an experiment designed to improve and refine. It's time to let go of the past and move towards tomorrow's world. The so-called good old days were never all that good.

WE DON'T WANT CULTURAL CHANGE. WE'RE NOT READY TO CHANGE OUR MINDSET. WE DON'T WANT TO CHANGE ANYTHING.

Consultants are often asked to do only half of the job for which we were hired. Companies want us to implement only the mechanics and refrain from making any deep systemic changes. We are not supposed to question the status quo or attempt to change it. We are hired to do just enough to allow certain people to say: *We have done what was necessary. Now we can call it x,y,z, and the rest needs to be done by the employees. We have changed enough to give our employees the perfect working environment.* This attitude makes me want to throw my laptop out of the window.

[45] "Why We Hate Being Told What to Do." Pessimists Archive [podcast]. Accessed 28 June 2020. https://pessimists.co/why-we-hate-being-told-what-to-do/

I worked with one company that, instead of allowing us to streamline its process through cooperation and collaboration, permitted us only to add a few meetings, which were primarily jours fixes. In this sense, the company was not unique. As more bureaucracy was required to administer these new events, ultimately, all we achieved was to preserve the worst aspects of the company, and to pile more events and bureaucracy on top of them. We were going in circles.

We were able to make changes only at the team level, without changing anything in the structure of the company. Making foundational changes was the only way to remove the root cause and have a sustainable, long lasting effect. This was out of reach. We were allowed to make changes within the teams, but it was already a challenge just to align the teams with each other. Various external vendors were staffing the teams, which served as black boxes.

Companies should be addressing change as part of strategic discussions.

No wonder many people think of organisational change as just another trend that won't stick. It's only a matter of time until it becomes outmoded, like so many other trends have in the past. Companies are willing to change things and try out new initiatives, as long as it doesn't pose any risk to middle management. That's where the real power lies.

WHAT TO CONSIDER OR TRY NOW

- **When** incorporating change, it may be helpful to apply some tactics taken from the field of behavioural psychology. Ask yourself the following questions:

  ☑ Are we ready? Can we do it? Do we have the resources and knowledge to successfully make a lasting change?

  ☑ Is there anything standing in our way? What is preventing us from changing?

  ☑ Which aspects and benefits of the old way of doing things appeal to us than those of the new way? What might trigger a return to our former patterns and behaviour?

- **When** driving change, it's best to identify barriers and frame conditions early on in the process. Based on these, be clear about whether or not you wish to proceed. If yes, communicate what is achievable. When you start, be fully committed to making it work.

- **Create** a detailed as-is overview of your change journey by using a lean change canvas,[46] which helps you gather important factors and analyse its dependencies (such as urgency, ideal stat, success criteria, change recipients, and so on).

- **Utilise** a lightweight planning approach such as lean change management,[47] which guides you, via a strategic change canvas, to evaluate various change options, experiment, and continuously adjust your trajectory towards your targets.

- **Letting** people participate in creating change can help to overcome their resistance to it. Therefore, co-create the change.

---

[46] "Create a New Lean Change Canvas." Canvanizer. Accessed 29 Aug. 2020. https://canvanizer.com/new/lean-change-canvas

[47] Little, Jason. "What Is Lean Change Management?" Lean Change Management. Accessed 24 July 2020. https://leanchange.org/lean-change-management-3/

- **To successfully** enact change, ask yourself the following questions:

  ☑ **Are we able to change?** Are we ourselves prepared for change? Do we have the necessary tools, skills, support, training, guidance and coaching?

  ☑ **Are we allowed to change?** Is our organisation prepared for change? Are there any elements external to ourselves (e.g., incentive systems, bosses) hindering us? Have all levels of the hierarchy been informed about the change and are they willing to participate in enacting it? Are there bonus systems in place to incentivise individuals to support the change?

  ☑ **Do we want to change?** Is it desirable to change? Is there a benefit and do I see the benefit? Has the organisation presented a convincing story and credible reasons?

GETTING WORK DONE IS MORE IMPORTANT THAN TREATING PEOPLE WITH RESPECT AND DIGNITY.

A company asked me to help them implement a new way of working that would involve fewer hierarchies, encourage employees to be more proactive, and place more value on teamwork than on individual contribution. It was hoped that the latter would create a culture in which people would prioritise the success of the team over their personal advancement.

Although I was given a certain amount of latitude, particular constraints in the roles and responsibilities of some people in one department were to remain in place. These were to include:

- Team lead responsibilities
- Stand-duty during the night and weekend
- Access to specific applications and systems in use
- Alignments with business areas for new requirements
- Implementation and changes being performed on mission critical systems

The company had simply started a new project, in addition to the ones already running. New responsibilities were also added to the current ones. You can imagine the excitement of all those involved.

We should have had all hands on deck. Ideally, everyone would contribute their skills, intellect and domain know-how to this new project without being too distracted by carrying out the aforementioned responsibilities as well. When initiating any new project certain arrangements have to be made (e.g., for time-tracking, office preparations, meeting schedule, responsibilities, trainings). In this case, the priorities for implementation were outlined, and the company's policies (e.g., budgeting rules, contracts for external vendors) and its internal politics were taken into account.

A number of employees were fully deployed to the project, while others were assigned to devote to it a specific percentage of their available time. I can recall that certain individuals were supposed to dedicate 27.5 percent of their time to the project. This number has been burned into my memory forever, purely because it is hilariously specific. This, in itself, should have set off alarm bells.

The employees were to follow the reporting protocol that had always been in place. This meant that some people were reporting to project managers that were new to them, while others were still reporting to their old line managers. Certain individuals were to be freed up as soon as possible, in case they were urgently needed by their former teams, even though they were supposed to be working 100 percent on the current project.

This was when I first became acquainted with the term *head monopolies*, which refers to people who are unique in terms of solving problems within their teams and will, therefore, always be called back. The way that this organisation simply moved these employees around betrayed a lack of respect for their dignity and sense of purpose. How could these individuals be expected to maintain their motivation or the sense that they could truly improve anything in that company?

The Project Management Institute has published a thoughtful article about this topic on their blog.[48] Human beings need the following six elements to feel fulfilled in their work lives:

- a sense of certainty and safety in the current environment
- variety and uncertainty, in the sense of being able to move between various tasks, and still being surprised by learning and possibilities
- love and connection, through bonding with other people and teams

---

[48] Ciccotti, Kevin. "The Human Factor in Project Management." Paper presented at PMI® Global Congress 2014—North America, Phoenix, AZ. Newtown Square, PA: Project Management Institute. https://bit.ly/2RMpMZM

- a sense of significance, both professionally and personally, through recognition of their work and a sense of being needed
- growth in terms of development and learning
- contribution in terms of being able to share and add value

WHAT TO CONSIDER OR TRY NOW

- **Start** taking these steps to increase your truck factor and reduce head monopolies:

  - ☑ Pair other team members with the expert to work alongside them and gain the appropriate knowledge and skills that way, instead of communicating that information in writing.

  - ☑ Remove the expert from their dedicated team and appoint them as an advisor to teams needing his expertise. This positions many members of all of these teams to gain the required knowledge.

- **Watch out** for matrixed structures or the need to report to several managers and supervisors. This comes often with working in parallel, including partial project assignments. Avoid or minimize this.

- **Avoid** being delegated and temporary deployment based on linear organisational structures that result in people having to answer to two bosses at once. Even if one boss is on leave, the person will still have to answer to that person when they return.

- **Watch out:** while being an expert yourself seems to be desirable it can also be a dead end when the knowledge becomes irrelevant.

WE'D APPRECIATE YOUR HELP WITH THIS, BUT PLEASE DON'T CHANGE ANYTHING.

These days, assessments are very much in vogue. It makes sense, as before you change anything, you need to have an idea of what is working and what isn't. While it is not necessarily a new concept, the difference is that in the past, clients simply walked around the office and tried to get an overview of their area of responsibility, whereas nowadays they outsource this task to experts. Because of this, it would seem that the client—usually represented by a department lead—is forced to optimise the status quo within their department. Regardless of whether they are new to the position or the organisation, or whether they have been doing this job for quite a while, they all request external support to be covered.

In one of these projects the following happened. I spent many nights researching and preparing to discuss and clarify my opinions and recommendations and to thoroughly back them up with supporting arguments. As much as I hoped that all of this would be useful and constructive for the client, I hoped that the discussions themselves would be fruitful. As well as addressing the issues at hand, I always hope the conversation will give rise to some new thoughts and ideas that may provoke real change in the organisation.

With time, it gradually dawned on me that none of my suggestions would ever be implemented. All of this effort was made for the sole purpose of allowing everyone to keep doing exactly what they had always done, but with their backs covered. None of the people involved were willing to break their habits or modify their behaviour; they wanted only to prove to the higher-ups that they had done everything within their means. *Something is wrong at the company, and now we have it in writing. An expert has said it was not our fault; someone else is to blame.* They would use the assessment as a shield to deflect blame onto other departments. Their chosen strategy was to blunder through this mess and hope for better times. This is the game many companies are playing these days. I must say, it is an expensive one.

WHAT TO CONSIDER OR TRY NOW

■ **Assess** a situation by incorporating all types of information: both first-hand (behavioural; in writing) and second-hand (anecdotal; opinions; guesses). Examine relevant stakeholders and hierarchies

■ **Be aware** of the fact that as long as you're getting paid by someone else, you are dependent on them in some way. This reduces your options and your sphere of influence, including the freedom to speak up.

■ **Learn** how to provide constructive feedback. There are several models for how to structure this. The one I like relates back to the work on non-violent communication by Marshall Rosenberg, who defined a feedback model comprising four steps: (1) state what you have observed or perceived; (2) describe how it makes you feel; (3) explain the needs or values underlying why this is important; (4) make your request for change.[49]

■ **Let go** of the need to be liked. Being the nice guy won't help you get things done. You will need to nag and nurture, which may make you unpopular. Sometimes you are simply hired for that. Make your peace with it.

---

[49] Bailey, Dave. "How to Deliver Constructive Feedback in Difficult Situations." Medium 8 April 2019 https://bit.ly/3fZpfO1

I'LL READ THE PAPER FOR TWO HOURS, SMOKE A CIGARETTE, GO TO LUNCH, DO A SPOT OF WORK, AND LEAVE EARLY.

This describes a typical workday for Dillon, as well as for many managers and company executives I have met. One of them is Dillon's superior, Mickey, the middle manager.

Mikey Middle-Manager - Quite smart because he definitely knows how to play the corporate game; for his own benefits.

Mickey is fond of saying: *Our staff is our greatest attribute.* However, he couldn't actually tell you who anyone is or what they actually do. If only Mickey would step out of his corner office, he could stop managing and actually learn to lead. It is not enough to delegate and command others to do your bidding; you must lead by example, work closely with your staff, and be fully engaged with what is happening at every level of your organisation.

Break up silos without creating new silos.

In too many companies, the various divisions and departments operate as silos. In such an insular environment, employees lose focus and drive, and nothing comes along to reset or recalibrate them.

While Dillon's indifference may be one symptom of a problem deep within the organisation that begins with the leadership, his inactivity is indefensible. There are many things that Dillon could do for himself, including reading and researching within his field, inciting change in his department or spending more time with colleagues who might inspire him. A good first step would be to talk to other people and gain some new insight instead of waiting for something great to happen.

What separates managers from leaders is that leaders work *with* their staff rather than letting their staff work *for* them. A true leader understands that people need to be challenged if they are to keep growing; makes sure there is an organisational growth plan in place to enable employees to envision a future that's different from their past and their present; proactively nurtures the wellbeing and career development of the people in their organisations; and rewards people for taking risks and initiating change, instead of standing in the way.

Think of the health of your project just like the body-mass index (BMI) – A Bureaucracy Management Index of more than app. 25% is considered unhealthy.

I've worked with so many companies who are floundering or stagnating because they have too many managers and not enough leaders. I've advised them to adjust their perspective and gradually implement the above changes. Years later, those who have failed to do so remain in the same quandary and have the same outlook.

WHAT TO CONSIDER OR TRY NOW

- **Ask** yourself whether you are a manager or a leader.[50] A leader must understand how to communicate and inspire; a manager needs to have the ability to coordinate, structure, plan, and analyse.

- **Leaders** tend to focus more on people and managers are more task oriented. This is often amplified by the system in which we work. If the organisation operates according to a target system that favours setting KPIs, this breeds an envi-

---

[50] Arruda, William. "Nine Differences Between Being a Leader and a Manager." *Forbes.* 15 Nov. 2016. https://bit.ly/3kMyogh

ronment in which profit and growth are valued above learning and fulfilment.

■ **A true** leader cares about people. Common capabilities include coaching people; a humancentric style of management; creating an environment where different styles can flourish; removing obstacles; facilitating open and honest communication; sharing an inspiring vision.

LET'S DECENTRALISE DECISION MAKING - BUT ONLY IF YOU COME UP WITH SOMETHING I AGREE WITH, OBVIOUSLY.

In 2016, the *Guardian* published an article about the early childhood education system in Finland. At the time, many countries in Europe were looking to take their cues from the Finnish education system. The secret to its success is thought to be rooted in its approach to early years education, which includes a Montessori-like approach that emphasises explorative play and social development, and delays formal education in reading, writing and mathematics until the age of seven.[51] The article implies that simply copying and pasting these elements to education systems in other countries will not have the desired effect without understanding and adopting the philosophy underlying them and changing things at a deeper level.

Merely borrowing a few tools from the toolbox and applying them within a different context without fully understanding the whole system is a clear path to failure. When a system works, several elements are working together within a certain environment to make it successful. Some aspects may not be recognised as primary success factors but play a huge part overall.

We see this happening all the time in the corporate setting. One such practice, out of a set of working principles, is to decentralise decision making. Let people take responsibility and ownership at the level where the situation actually occurs. In theory, this all seems great. The reality is that many managers are not truly prepared to decentralise decision making—they are only comfortable using it as a way to delegate tasks or responsibilities. Or, they are prepared to let others speak up, but that is all.

---

[51] Butler, Patrick. "No grammar school, lots of play: the secrets of Europe's top education system." *The Guardian* online. 20 Sept. 2016. https://bit.ly/31SLLTz

It goes something like this. Mickey, the middle manager, appoints someone else to make a decision. If the appointed person presents the decision that Mickey wants to put forth, he will applaud this person's decision-making process, thus giving the impression that the decision-making process has been decentralised. If Mickey doesn't agree with the decision, he will question the decision-making process until he runs this person into the ground. It will be understood that the person has failed to adequately defend their choice, and now Mickey is forced to take matters into his own hands and make the final decision.

You are ready to decentralise decision making only when you are ready to accept decisions that challenge your biases.

In both outcomes, Mickey has done exactly as he initially intended, except that he has gone through the rigmarole of pretending to decentralise the decision-making process. As long as middle managers like Mickey are not ready to trust their colleagues with the autonomy to make decisions, any attempt to decentralise decision making will simply be a time-consuming charade that demeans employees and may erode their respect in the long run.

WHAT TO CONSIDER OR TRY NOW

■ **Understand** that due to the layered and interconnected system of values within a particular culture, there is a complex interplay between principles, actions and behaviours. Therefore, an initiative that had one outcome in a specific setting will not necessarily produce the same outcome when applied in a different setting. There is a good read about the attempt to copy the Toyota car production system (also called Lean Manufacturing) when transferring it to the New United Motor Manufacturing, Inc. (NUMMI) factory in the US, as it is an interesting story that clearly illustrates the above point.[52] To summarise what happened, a defunct General Motors plant was reopened as a joint venture between GM and Toyota to manufacture vehicles for both brands. GM employees were sent to Toyota's Takaoka plant to learn its lean manufacturing method. All its tools, machines, processes, methods, checklists and roles were copied wholesale, seemingly without any critical thinking or necessary adjustments.

■ **Instead of** simply copying solutions from other contexts or environments, try to find the root cause of the problem. Ask yourself why. When you come up with an answer, keep digging deeper by asking yourself why. Repeat this process until you reach the source of the issue.[53]

■ **Jurgen Appelo's** Delegation Poker[54] provides a useful model for decentralising decision making with clear rules (when there is a way to override the rules and when there isn't) by outlining seven levels of delegation, ranging from (1) "I tell you without any contribution by anyone" to (7) "I fully delegate without knowing anything on the issue." For each re-

[52] Sloan, John. "How to Change a Culture: Lessons from NUMMI ."
MITSloan Management Review. Winter 2010, vol. 51, no. 2. https://bit.ly/3g2ozHD

[53] "Five whys." Wikipedia. Last modified 15 Sept. 2020.
https://en.wikipedia.org/wiki/Five_whys

[54] "Delegation Poker & Delegation Board." Management 3.0.
Accessed 29 Aug. 2020. https://bit.ly/2Emcq3p

curring decision within an environment, one of these seven levels can be derived via this method, which helps the team and the management to determine with mutual biasing which level each of the involved parties deems suitable.[55]

- **It's helpful** to understand exactly how everything is connected. Systems thinking[56] is an integrative approach that utilises tools, such as mental models and causal loop diagrams, to help you visualise complex problems and environments.

- **We mentioned** already Intentional / Intent-based leadership as modern way to lead knowledge workers. It is a way to increase self-organisation or decentralized decision making. In order to successfully apply this technique, consider the competence and skills of the person, the willingness to take over and the clarity of the intent / delegation.

[55] Appelo, Jurgen. "The 7 Levels of Delegation." *Medium.* 25 Feb. 2015. https://bit.ly/3mHVwO9

[56] Kim, Daniel. "Introduction to Systems Thinking." Systems Thinker. Accessed 24 July 2020. https://bit.ly/31Z1eI2

THIS WILL NEVER WORK IN OUR COMPANY. I HAVE BEEN HERE LONG ENOUGH TO KNOW WHAT WILL OR WON'T WORK.

As consultants, we often hear this: *Even though the practice you've suggested has been proven to work for many different companies, these must have been smaller, a different sector and less complex—or even start-ups. It won't work for us.*

People working in companies are often fond of the notion that the company's success is a result of its uniqueness, which is embodied in an incredibly complicated structure and the complex processes that helped it to succeed. Hence the principles and practices that work for all those other companies out there will not work for this particular company. This company requires a specialised solution. Part of my job is to strip away this belief, which borders on superstition, and to convince companies to stop spending so much intellectual capital on procedures and rituals that waste time and resources instead of directing it toward revenue-generating, customer-focused products.

> Money spent on the product, culture and optimizing processes is money well spent unless you're re-inventing the wheel with every project.

It doesn't make sense to spend money and time on individualised procedures and different operating models for every new project that is being started within the company. Rather than establishing new working protocols every other month, which wastes resources, it is preferable to establish, once and for all, an operating model (comprising a set culture and system of principles, values, ethics as well as structures and processes) that is consistent throughout the company or at least across departments. This can be upgraded and tweaked every now and again instead of being rebuilt from scratch every half year.

Once I am able to get these points across, people let go of the preconceptions they have internalised, and they begin to hear me. The first battle is always to deconstruct these deeply entrenched practices, principles, behaviours and role descriptions.

They start to fight me on every point. Various people take it upon themselves to gently remind me that they have been here much longer than I have and understand the company much better than I ever will. They seem to forget that my newness is why they hired me—someone who can see the forest for the trees. We always get there in the end, given enough time.

This coaching process often involves chasing people around in an effort to get them to answer my questions, since these people are always in a rush. They're already focusing on the next thing, without having fully grasped the current opportunity or challenge at hand. I fully appreciate that it isn't easy to ask for help, get out of one's comfort zone, and open one's mind to new ideas. After all, this is the outlook that has led the company to where it finds itself today—in desperate need of help.

WHAT TO CONSIDER OR TRY NOW

■ **Make** clear in which domain your expertise is based and where your focus lies, so as to avoid telling someone with upwards of twenty years of professional experience how to do his job. For example, if you want to advocate on Agile methods (lightweight methods with small increments for getting early feedback), make clear that the gain lies in applying your state-of-the-art methodical know-how to this specific company environment.

■ **Build** your credibility by sharing your personal examples and stories from your own experience. Even if you believe the method you advocate is simply the greatest thing on earth, people need to see evidence-based proof.

■ **Vote** for a culture of openness, experimentation, and an attitude of *What if? What if this would work?* Try teaming up with a domain expert who can support you in presenting a convincing example case.

■ **Don't** expect to change a company's culture right at the outset. Start by changing behaviours and instilling new habits and patterns. You don't change someone's thinking by preaching or teaching but by generating new experiences based on actions taken.

WE NEED TO INTERNALLY TRANSFER KNOWLEDGE, SO WE HAD BETTER APPOINT A KNOWLEDGE MANAGER.

I was hired to help out with one project, on which I worked with the person responsible for taking the decisions and steering the organisation. We were on good terms from the beginning, and our discussions were fruitful. Whatever point we discussed, we always came to an understanding. This person's fatal flaw was that whenever advice was offered, he gratefully accepted it. I often was reminded of a puppet.

Paul Puppet - in charge, but helpless.
Does everything you tell him. But please don't let him on his own.

When no advice was given, which sometimes occurred, as no one can shadow a person 100 percent of the time, he slipped back into old habits and behaviours that were counterproductive.

Many external people were involved within the project setup. A command was given to appoint certain key personnel—meaning internal employees—to positions that were crucial for the project. This would offer these employees many advantages, including a great career plan and development opportunities, as well as the possibility to lead teams consisting of internal and external personnel. This manner of project steering was easier, since no external politics were involved and all parties at the table had the same goal, which was to make the company successful while spending as little money as possible or to finish early or on time.

Paul Puppet tended to take decisions even when he hadn't been advised. Instead of putting internal personnel into place, as requested; he appointed externals. This was swiftly communicated, and contracts were drawn up. Everything happened so quickly that there was no opportunity to react and change course. In the meantime, he became convinced of the urgency of the situation, as he was advised to put the internal people into the positions, because: *otherwise they will not be available anymore and our intellectual capital will be lost.*

It was about intellectual capital all along, but instead of making the choice wisely and strategically with a long-term solution in mind, the decision was taken in a short-sighted manner. When I sat down with him to address the issue of internal knowledge transfer, the first solution he offered was to take care of this issue in one to two years. Clearly, this was not an option. The second solution he proposed was to install a knowledge manager, who would be responsible for running around gathering information and sharing it with the rest of the company.

"We can't solve problems by using the same kind of thinking we used when we created them.
-Albert Einstein

Within this legendary suggestion, can you guess where the flaw was perceived to be? To whom shall the knowledge manager transfer this knowledge? And who might we appoint as the knowledge manager? Why can't we give them a proper position on the project right away, instead of side-lining them? The answer came: *We don't have time for this now. We don't have the people with the relevant skillset available right now. We would first need to build it up.* In that case, I would suggest that they start building it up immediately. The project would be the ideal place for that. Why waste any more valuable time?

WHAT TO CONSIDER OR TRY NOW

- **Although** it is helpful to conduct some research to help inform your decision, having to process a vast amount of (often contradictory) information, may leave you feeling confused. To keep from becoming overwhelmed, you can organise your thoughts by keeping a list of your top five supporting facts. Try to stick to a maximum of five key points. As you go along, you can always strike out the less important ones.

- **Use** these steps to shape and harden a decision. Imagine you're in a situation with the need to take an important decision. Now pretend you have already taken the decision and imagine how you would tell and defend this choice one by one to various individuals: a parent, a teacher, your supervisor, and so on. Then carry out the same exercise defending an alternative decision or a variation. Choose people who think differently than you do and who might not have the same opinion as you do.

- **Create** a spreadsheet[57] or a decision table. Along one axis, you can mark the various options. Along the other axis, write down the factors used for evaluating effectiveness or success. The areas where options and assessment criteria intersect can be graded (e.g., low, medium or high impact).

---

[57] Pinola, Melanie. "Make Better Quality Decisions with the Help of this Spreadsheet." 25 January 2012. https://bit.ly/2Y3xGS2

06 | CULTURE EATS STRATEGY FOR BREAKFAST

W HEN, IN A BUSINESS CONTEXT, SOMEONE ASKS YOU FOR HELP, it feels good. Not just good—it feels great. Your reputation has preceded you. You were hired on the strength of your LinkedIn profile or a glowing word-of-mouth recommendation. You feel that your skills and expertise are appreciated. The same is true when you're hired for a job or a project. Then, as soon as you show up and start doing the work you've been enlisted to carry out, the people involved begin to lose interest.

You ask yourself: *What has caused this sudden change of heart? Was it something I said?*

Yes, absolutely. In most cases, you will have asked the company to implement some changes. People generally do not love this.

But isn't that precisely what you have been hired to do? Well, yes and no. Many companies hire consultants in the hopes that we will provide plug-and-play solutions. Simply plug it in and switch it on.

No such solution exists. The truth is that every little thing you want to change threatens to turn their working environment upside down or unearth emerging internal talent, which either questions their decision making or, worse, shows that poor judgment has been applied in the past.

As a catalyst for change, you'll encounter resistance in every form, from those at every level. You'll do well to familiarise yourself with the various objections you'll hear from organisations and individuals. It is important to be aware of how such concerns can provide convenient excuses to procrastinate change.

1 | There is something else more urgent we need to take care of first.

As real change takes time, there will always be something else that takes priority. To override this objection, you will need to prove that there is an imminent need for change and that the organisation would do well to prioritise it.

2 | How much time, money and people will we be required and what kind of return can we expect?

These are difficult, if not impossible, to forecast and quantify. If the company insists on seeing some concrete figures before they will even agree to start the process, things can stall out indefinitely. Encourage them to keep a flexible mindset. Make sure you stick to managing expectations rather than making promises you may not be able to keep.

3 | We are already cutting things so close that we cannot afford to dip into the valley of despair.

The company may say that right now, they can't afford the downtime associated with change, so they will do it when they can afford the downtime. That time will never come. As demonstrated in the Satir Change Model, change always involves periods of chaos and recovery, and things have to get worse before they can get better.[58]

[58] Smith, Steven M. "The Satir Change Model." 4 October 1997. Steven M. Smith (personal website). https://bit.ly/2FQd223

4 | **My entire career is based on the very process you are proposing to change. Will I be able to adjust to this new world?**

Managers have the power to change the status quo, but as the status quo serves them and protects their job security, there is little incentive for them to change it. Another related attitude often encountered: *I am the manager here, so anything new around here should be invented by me or led by me.* Can we expect to see anything truly innovative or ground-breaking from someone so deeply entrenched in the system?

5 | **Don't disturb my peace. You are paying me enough to operate in default mode and nothing more.**

Due to a lack of job satisfaction or personal incentive, the employee prefers to remain on cruise control and is unwilling to spare enough bandwidth to absorb any new information.

THIS DOES NOT MATCH MY JOB DESCRIPTION.

I was particularly struck by one particular scene in the Steve Jobs biopic. When the Macintosh project stalls, Jobs sets out to recruit the company's best minds to work on his team. We see him running around inside the Apple headquarters. *Andy Herzberg! I've heard you're awesome and skilled with code. Only the best people work on the Macintosh project. You have to be part of the team. Get your stuff and follow us.* No one sits down to discuss roles and responsibilities. Focus and purpose come first. Just get the right people and they'll get the job done. Mind blown.

Although role descriptions are useful, we can't let them define us. Being cross-functional is a key aspect of working together. Having people with different skills, experiences and viewpoints on the team brings a range of perspectives to the table.

I worked with a company who had long been entrenched in a rigid hierarchical structure. Every role was delineated with a very long and detailed list of responsibilities, each meticulously explained. They had in place a career model outlined with clearly defined stages, and the scale of pay, which varied according to the path and level of your current position. At this time, I was helping them to implement a new way of working, which required transcending the constraints imposed by stringently defined duties and hierarchies by casting off the structure underlying seniority and handovers. The whole idea was to try to bridge the gaps and work together as a team—to really collaborate. In this climate, all team members were expected to pitch in and work together, and to learn to approach their roles and responsibilities in a more fluid and flexible way.

Old habits die hard, and one particular situation arose where the old mentality came shining through. We had to do some requirements engineering in the area of a particular use case for front-desk personnel. After a few days, we figured out some of the people involved weren't doing anything at all to support the project. They said things like: *This kind of work isn't in my job description. This colleague over there works in analytics, and he earns more than I do, so he should be the one to do it.*

We asked these people what they were doing in the meantime. *Nothing. As I'm not being paid to do the other job, it's not my problem. I'll just read the newspaper or tidy my desk until he has sorted it out.*

The one person who was actually working on the project was clearly under great deal of strain. Meanwhile, not more than a few metres away, three of his colleagues were sitting around doing absolutely nothing. Needless to say, I was appalled. I asked myself: *Will these people ever really work together as a team? Where does this insular attitude come from?* It seems to me that job descriptions and guidelines, as well as outdated career models, may have stamped out the adaptability and resourcefulness of this generation of employees.

WHAT TO CONSIDER OR TRY NOW

- **Although** it isn't easy to change deeply ingrained habits, science shows that this is possible even at an advanced age, given the right process.[59] Think of a bad habit or pattern you'd like to unlearn, and replace it with a good habit.

- **Job** descriptions can be constrictive, as they put people in boxes. By defining people's roles in rigid terms, you may limit their outlook, behaviour and development. Try phrasing job descriptions using an open-ended language that allows for more freedom and adaptability. You may wish to expand upon the following concepts of non-traditional/more modern roles:[60]

---

[59] Fishbane, Monica. "Why Change is So Hard: The Power of Habit in the Human Brain. Good Therapy. https://bit.ly/30Z91QJ

[60] Baker, Tim. "Is It Time to Kill the Job Description?" 27 February 2017. *HRM*. https://bit.ly/2CA8SKc

☑ Positive mental attitude and enthusiasm role, or growth mindset.[61] I recommend checking out Carol Dweck's Mindset: The New Psychology of Success.

☑ Team role. To learn how to build strong and dimensional teams, I suggest taking a look at Dr Meredith Belbin's research on the elementary team roles.[62]

☑ Skill development role. This could well describe a team lead or manager or any kind of people manager within a matrixed organisation. Is it present; is it working; are these people where they need to be; do they have the methods and skills to drive skill development? Try out the concept of Communities of Practice (CoP) and appoint a coordinator or leader to drive this.[63]

☑ Innovation and continuous improvement role. This role is deeply ingrained when using lean or Agile methodologies. They stress continuous improvement also often referred to as even relentless improvement. Within one Agile framework called "Scrum" one role, the Scrum Master, oversees learning and improvement.[64]

---

[61] Dweck, Carol. "What Having a 'Growth Mindset' Actually Means." 13 January 2016. Harvard Business Review. https://bit.ly/342NnNq

[62] "The Nine Belbin Team Roles." Belbin. Accessed 24 July 2020. https://bit.ly/2Fprai9

[63] Miller, Richard. "Building a Successful Community of Practice." Miller-Klein Associates, Ltd. 2006 https://bit.ly/3atVWC2

[64] What Is a Scrum Master: Learn About the Role of the Scrum Master." Scrum.org. Accessed 24 July 2020. https://www.scrum.org/resources/what-is-a-scrum-master

OUR ONLY CONCERN IS THE BOTTOM LINE.
NOTHING ELSE MATTERS.

Our next character is Bonny. She is the boss. It doesn't matter whether she's the boss of her department or of the whole organisation, as long as we understand that Bonny is primarily concerned with results.

Bonny Boss - looking for results.
Financials and results matter to her. People, not so much.

Once in a while, it's possible to get through to her and convince her of certain aspects or even to explain your side of things. But most of the time, she is all about results and outcomes. She tends to view people primarily as resources. When I approached Bonny to discuss certain aspects of the project, she communicated directly that money is her top priority. She wants things to be as cheap as they can be.

Money is a good tool but a poor objective. Reflect upon what really gives meaning to your life and work.

Now, we've all heard of professional athletes turning down offers of higher salaries and more perks to sign or stay with their favourite teams. A player may have a sentimental attachment to a particular club for whatever reason. Perhaps they love the home city or their family members and friends live there. They may wish to see their home team succeed. In any case, such decisions are based upon a purpose other than merely making as much money as possible.

To some extent, this can apply to ordinary professions, such as consulting. Consultants on a fixed monthly salary generally have working hours that fall somewhere between fixed and slightly flex ible. For those who are self-employed, their earnings are more directly dependent on the daily rates they receive from the client. For clients like Bonny, negotiating contracts and daily rates bear more importance than the quality she receives. I wanted to broach this topic with her but didn't have the chance to do so.

When negotiating contracts, it goes without saying that the financial aspect is an important factor. But this shouldn't outweigh the purpose. When negotiations are primarily focused on pushing down the price, often the quality and scope of work will go down as well. This also works the other way. A company may try to drive the price as high as it possibly can, without increasing the scope or quality of the service or product it provides. Ultimately, this defeats the purpose, as eventually the client will switch to a competitor who provides the same service or product at a cheaper price.

If you succeed in pushing down the price, nobody wins. Nothing comes for free, and you get what you pay for. Let's say you have

> If you succeed in pushing down the price, nobody wins.

a longstanding and trusted partnership with a certain company. You start to push the company for more deliverables or higher quality. If the company agrees to meet your demands at the same price as before, what would you think? Either the company was overcharging or underperforming before or there will be shortcomings in the deliverables.

Because clients like Bonny would rather not pay premium rates and will often choose the cheapest offer without considering quality, consultancies try to carve out as much as they can, which is only possible if you hire less qualified (or less experienced) staff and impose impossibly tight timeframes. We have all seen the young professional clad in a brand-new suit, sitting in a boardroom, and spouting rather vague answers and suggestions. He or she certainly looks the part and speaks like a textbook but has little experience of dealing with real-life situations and putting the theory into practice. Projects drag on and meander aimlessly for years.

Therein lies the problem. It's not enough to agree on the price. Clients and consultants must be on the same page when it comes to the desired outcome and purpose of the work. In the long run, cutting corners to save money proves to be a false economy for all parties involved. The consultant may end up losing the client, and the client incurs more expense if they have to hire someone else to go back and fix the issues that weren't addressed the first time around. Moreover, being forced to switch horses midstream may compromise the quality of the end result. When people are so eager to get started on a project that they focus all their energy on securing the budget and getting things rolling, they often fail to put in the proper planning and preparation required to produce world-class results.

Far better to work hand in hand from the outset, bringing in qualified experts and allocating adequate time to achieve truly astounding work. The purpose should be to spend our time wisely, with the aim of creating a worthwhile result that fulfils the original vision to its utmost potential.

WHAT TO CONSIDER OR TRY NOW

- **Learn** some strategies for dealing with people who are result oriented and driven, thus called drivers.[65]

  ☑ Respect their time. Be prepared and get straight to the point.

  ☑ Stick to the facts. Avoid discussing rumours, estimates, feelings, and intuition. Instead, quote statistics, studies, reports, and concrete information.

  ☑ Prove your competence and credibility through facts, milestones and achievements.

  ☑ Let them retain a modicum of control. Allow for some give and take in all of your transactions with them.

  ☑ Follow up on your promises. Earn their trust through your performance. Keep deadlines and commitments.

- **Ask** yourself whether money is the most important factor in your work life and whether it makes you happy. What gives your life meaning? Searching for meaning in your life is the way to find happiness. Do not target happiness itself, as this is abstract and can only be tentative. The Japanese concept of ikigai refers to one's reason for being.[66] Try to discover yours. Talk to a friend to help organise your thoughts. If you like to read, you may wish to dive into some of John Strelecky's work.[67] In particular, I'd recommend The Big Five for Life.

- **Think** about what drives you and why. This will help you to be more fulfilled in your work and life and also help you to understand how to motivate others. Research various theories and interpretations. A good starting point is Drive: The

[65] "Social Style®: The Driving Social Style." TRACOM. Accessed 24 July 2020. https://bit.ly/2DYYk7Q

[66] García, Héctor. *Ikigai: The Japanese Secret to a Long and Happy Life.* Penguin, 2017.

[67] Strelecky, John (personal website). Accessed 24 July 2020. https://www.johnstrelecky.com/books/

Surprising Truth About What Motivates Us, in which Daniel Pink argues that we are motivated by intrinsic values[68].He has consolidated decades of work on motivation in his book. Additionally, and very known you can relate to the corresponding 10 minute RSA animate YouTube clip.

- **It is** also worth checking out Jurgen Appelo's game Moving Motivators.[69] Based on extensive research on the topic of motivation, Appelo compiled a list of the ten intrinsic desires that inspire motivation. These can be memorised using the acronym CHAMPFROGS (as seen below).

Curiosity, **H**onour, **A**cceptance, **M**astery, **P**ower, **F**reedom, **R**elatedness, **O**rder, **G**oal, **S**tatus

You may find it helpful to perform a quick assessment of your primary motivators. On a scale of one to ten, rate how important each of these factors is to you or simply bring all of these ten in a linear order.

[68] Pink, Daniel H. *Drive: The Surprising Truth about What Motivates Us.* Riverhead Books, 2011.

[69] Appelo, Jurgen. *Management 3.0: Leading Agile Developers, Developing Agile Leaders.* Addison-Wesley Professional, 2011.

OUR VENDORS HAVE DIFFERENT CONTRACTS. SOME GET PAID FOR FINDING BUGS, SOME ARE BEING PAID FOR SOLVING THEM.

A colleague and I conducted a two-day software product development workshop. As the attendees came from various countries, the workshop was conducted in English. We introduced a particular method that involves breaking down the work into smaller chunks to enable the prioritisation of specific tasks and thus increase transparency during the process. This would include letting the client know as you introduce new features, troubleshoot bugs, carry out maintenance, and so on.

The workshop was attended mainly by managers, who would decide whether to sponsor this way of working and then introduce it to their colleagues, who would actually be working within this structure. Bonny also happened to attend parts of the workshop. We explained how the method works and presented the benefits, which are primarily to do with transparency. All the work that needs to be done should be visible and apparent so that it can be properly prioritised. Due to the time constraint, we didn't get into the aspects of change management. Anyway, we were addressing the people who were most likely to be negatively affected by the change.

Looking back on it now, I can see that we were somewhat naïve. A lively discussion ensued, during which the pitch of the voices increased, objections were raised, and speculations were made. The attendees addressed us in English with strong regional accents and sometimes spoke in their native languages, which we didn't understand.

At a certain point, Bonny took us aside and explained that her colleagues had been hired under various contracts. Most of them were not direct employees but were attending this workshop as representatives of their respective consulting companies. These companies had been working on the concrete project with our client for several months.

When working on a project with many facets, many companies get it wrong, despite having positive intentions. By the time I am called in, the project is being setup and therefore often set for failure. The focus is on adopting a different working approach, and no one is paying much attention to the people involved. Although the changes affect everyone, not everyone is fully informed. The employees start to make all kinds of assumptions, and this never ends well.

That's what was happening here. The contracts were already in place, and this was where the problem lay. We had explained that it is beneficial to come up with quotas for each type of work, the purpose being to establish that there would always be sufficient demand focused on features, which would serve to drive functionality and innovation, and to ensure that issues such as bugs and defects are also being addressed. This is fine, as long as there is a contract in place that supports these quotas. However, if a new contract would be drawn up whereby, let's say, the client company receives a discount proportional to the number of bugs found, this is obviously more favourable for the client company. The supplier would stand to lose quite a lot of money.

"A system must be managed. Left to themselves, components become selfish, competitive. We cannot afford the destructive effect of competition."

—W. Edwards Deming

Four vendors were in attendance at the workshop, and every single vendor had negotiated a different contract: the one we've already described; one that was a time-and-material contract; one that was all-inclusive regardless of how many bugs were found; and one that specified that the provider would fix a certain number of bugs per month for free, so that the client would pay only for any bugs in excess of that number.

Once we became aware of this, imagine our joy while listening to the ensuing hours of lively debate, conducted exclusively in a language we did not understand. This all transpired during the workshop, and the sheer panic in Bonny's eyes was a sight I'll never forget. She must have felt like she'd been caught cheating at poker. Someone in her position never finds it easy to cope with transparency.

Instead of everyone working together towards the shared ambition of building great products, the purpose and focus lies elsewhere. Depending on whom you ask, you receive different answers about the strength of the product, the state of progress, and the unity of the team. This is a rather sad state of affairs.

WHAT TO CONSIDER OR TRY NOW

- **Systems** thinking shows us that optimising the parts seldom optimises the whole.[70] First establish an overarching target, and never let the parts decide on their KPIs, metrics and optimisation without taking the other parts or the overall targets into consideration. As independent systems tend to optimise themselves towards their own goals, it is essential that someone is assigned this overarching role.

- **One** useful goal-setting framework is objectives and key results (OKR).[71] Beyond other favourable properties, it places the focus on deriving key results from overarching objectives in a participative and alignment fostering approach. Furthermore, it focuses on a limited number of objectives, breaking them down and measuring them in short time frames.

- **Keep** in mind that as a person who is external to the system, you can never be the one person to change the system. You can influence, irritate and stimulate the system. If the system doesn't react, you are likely not to blame.

---

[70] Heylighen, F. "The Problem of Suboptimisation." Modified 26 January 1999. Principia Cybernetica Web. https://bit.ly/3fYhUOD

[71] White, Sarah K. "What is OKR? A Goal-Setting Framework for Thinking Big."
4 September 2018. CIO. https://bit.ly/2Ftojov

ONE UNIQUE SELLING PROPOSITION FOR YOU AS AN EMPLOYEE IS TO UNDERSTAND HOW OUR COMPLEX ENVIRONMENT WORKS.

I worked with one company whose structure and processes were incredibly complicated. It took weeks for me to understand its way of operating to the point where I was able to start helping them. I would say I understood approximately 70 percent of its operating model, which proved to be a decent proportion. It certainly was useful when I was communicating with department leads, to whom I often had to explain or clarify the company's processes. Sadly, the majority of employees seemed to work only within their specific section of the process without questioning or understanding how it fits into the system as a whole, so their insight was confined to a particular area. I was told that this limitation was a result of the company's very complex environment. *These processes are creating a great set of products. Everything is integrated and works together cohesively.*

When I talked with other employees, a different story emerged. They spoke of their frustration at long onboarding times, having to wait ages for minor changes to be implemented, and sub-par end products. Cash cows aside, I am not sure where companies like this one will end up in the future. What will happen as soon as a competitor starts to challenge them?

When dealing with a company that's this set in its ways, you must provide a concrete example of a case that demonstrates why this kind of thinking is flawed and doomed to fail. Otherwise it will just keep going around in circles. It will keep making half-hearted attempts to implement change initiatives without altering its labyrinthine processes. As this is where the problem really lies, any initiatives will eventually fail.

You have some idea of what they are producing, how their processes operate, which obstacles they must overcome, and which people need to be handled. Taking into account how much time you'd have to spend on research, argumentation, and winning over key people within the company, how long do you think it would take to introduce a new idea or approach? Typically, employees will try something new only for so long before giving up.

People prefer to carry on doing what already works within a company, even when what works is neither the best nor the most effective approach. They are reluctant to take on the challenge of truly innovating, because doing so would require them to persuade others to change their perspective and attitudes. Sticking out their necks in this way differentiates them and positions them as outsiders, which could endanger their careers in the short term.

In recent years, disruptive innovation has mushroomed.[72] Established companies are innovating, and new, innovative companies are founded. The banking industry is being challenged by fintech companies. The automotive sector has competitors emerging from a technological area in software, as software companies are developing self-driving vehicles. New apps and products are developed and brought to market within an ever-shorter timescale. Markets are in turmoil. Brands emerge, only to vanish just as quickly as they had appeared. In the current climate, it is surprising that so many companies remain occupied primarily with themselves.

"The structure of any system designed by an organisation is isomorphic to the structure of the organisation."

—Conway's Law

---

[72] Christensen, Clayton M., Michael E. Raynor, and Rory McDonald. "What Is Disruptive Innovation?" *Harvard Business Review.* From Dec 2015 issue. https://hbr.org/2015/12/what-is-disruptive-innovation

WHAT TO CONSIDER OR TRY NOW

- **One** helpful behaviour for complex environments is creating transparency and a common understanding by providing appropriate visualisation of the circumstances: Gaining understanding on how things are going here via mapping out the flow and processes can be done by using value-stream mapping.[73] In a workshop setting you map out the process steps, the transitions and sometimes qualitative properties as defects occurring, throughput, average processing and waiting times of each process step. You do this with as many experts for the process steps you have in scope as you can get. You focus on consolidating the As-Is situation first. In a second step you may want to optimize and change for the better. To work with the resulting new process using again the principles of transparency and common understanding of the flow use the already earlier explained Kanban framework.

- **Streamline** a development process by minimising waste. Reduce the influence of the seven wastes of lean manufacturing: overproduction, inventory, motion, defects, over-processing, waiting, and transport.[74]

- **To paraphrase** Peter Kruse, an organisational psychologist and collective intelligence expert: The brain of any individual is necessarily limited. If organisations are managed only by a few humans at the top, the organisation's capabilities will consequently be limited. In a knowledge working environment, there must be bottom-up ways to participate in creating visions, defining processes, choosing how to work and how to reach targets.

---

[73] "Identify Value Streams and ARTs." SAFe: Scaled Agile® Last updated 28 September 2019. https://bit.ly/2GfMMxO

[74] "7 Wastes of Lean: How to Optimize Resources." Kanbanize. Accessed 27 July 2020. https://bit.ly/342fufr

WE TELL OUR CUSTOMERS HOW THEY SHOULD WORK WITH US.

As you will likely have experienced as you go about your daily business, when you try to change things or even just to flag up a problem, you often will find yourself reaching a dead end. Whether you are having an issue with your insurance policy or questioning the checkout process at your local supermarket, when you try to escalate the issue, you'll find yourself coming up against some resistance.

It seems that many companies fail to appreciate that they have many types of customers, each with their own preferences for how to interact with their products and services. How can so many companies be ignorant of the fact that interacting with their customers is one of the most important ways to build trust?

> Finding the root cause is the real lever for change, problem solving only addresses the symptoms.

One of the reasons for this is structural. As those individuals who have the possibility to drive change within the organisation will not benefit directly by doing so, there is no incentive for them to listen to the customers or give them what they want. Every employee should be empowered and driven to change the customer's perception of the company. Even small incremental changes make a difference, but all too often these are not recognised or valued.

Let's say you phone your customer service representative, Dillon. He is not motivated to fix the situation, because this is not in his job description. To resolve your problem, he would be required to invest some extra effort, which is above his paygrade and would slow him down in completing his tasks. As Dillon's work rate is the criteria for how much he gets paid, he just wants to get you off the line as quickly as possible and move onto the next case. Dillon's apathy stems from the fact that he knows how things work in the company. This is a very deeply rooted problem many companies have.

While Dillon knows that his manager, Mickey, has the power to solve your issue, Dillon is also aware that Mickey doesn't have any interest in helping you, because he has the typical mentality of those in middle management. Mickey is paid a comfortable salary for the work of his subordinates. In Mickey's eyes, making improvements will only create more work for him, which will slow him down from reaching his goals. Dillon knows that even if he were to escalate the issue to Mickey, because Mickey is so far up in the hierarchy that no practical issue will truly affect him, Mickey remains shrouded in bureaucracy, and nothing will ever truly change.

WHAT TO CONSIDER OR TRY NOW

- **Understand** that a customer-centric mindset is a crucial starting point. Looking at the story we heard about Dillon and Mikey it is not a question on "are we allowed" (e.g. if it's against policies) or "are we able" (e.g. missing skills) to do something. It is primarily about "do we want to do something"!

- **Your** main driver for improvement and change originates in a customer-centric view. Map out the so-called customer journey. A customer journey map shows the story of the customer's experience. It not only identifies key interactions that the customer has with the organization, but it also brings user's feelings, motivations and questions for each of the touchpoints. Analyse it and visualise it. In doing this you will understand the current processes your customer needs to deal with and his feelings in every step he makes.

- **Inform** yourself about methods such as empathy mapping to more fully understand your customer. Get familiar with how they live, eat, sleep, and breathe.

- **Your** next customer is not necessarily beyond your company. It may be someone you are already serving. That's why it's essential to maintain and nurture good internal customer relationships.

- **The lack** of an "improvement culture" is deeply ingrained in certain cultures. We can start to try to change it at the individual or team level. However, in the end it is culture that dominates what is promoted and what is suppressed.

- **Be aware** that even if the company you are dealing with is not customer-centric, there are already or there will be its competitors who get it.

YOU HAVE BEEN GIVEN ONE JOB, AND ONE JOB ONLY.

One might argue that the chain of command is helpful, as there is always a higher level within the hierarchy to handle escalations. But such structures do not always serve their intended purpose. In Edward Snowdon's book *Permanent Record,* he points out that when something had to be done about a particular situation in which he found himself, it was not sufficient to simply change the situation, because within the secret service, you are given one job, and one job only. That means you get one dedicated task. This one you have to follow up on. No creativity beyond it is allowed. Therefore, when Edward found out about major issues at the military academy he was attending, he informed his superior. After sending in two or three requests and having them rejected or ignored over three weeks, he notified his boss that he would be going over his head and informing the person higher up in the chain of command. You can imagine how well this went down with his boss and his boss's boss.

We see the same dynamic playing out when Dillon attempts to escalate any issue to his superior, Mickey. Middle managers similar to Mickey are persons of great importance, particularly in companies with complicated and deeply entrenched hierarchies. When we talk about change, transformation, evolution, and all that good stuff Mickey is a key figure.

As a gatekeeper, Mickey has the power to initiate change; however, he is unwilling to invest any extra time and money towards what he considers to be non-essential work. It also runs deeper than that. As someone who benefits from the status quo, Mickey has a vested interest in staving off change for as long as possible. He has invested a lot to reach his current position, and he did so with the specific objective of entrenching himself in the comfort of a familiar environment that includes stability, a routine, constant processes and a decent salary. Until a few years ago, middle management positions in large companies with smoothly running business models were the place to be for anyone whose mindset is similar to Mickey's. Therefore, Dillon's hands are tied.

This lack of insight on the part of leadership is inextricably linked with company hierarchies. The people who would take these decisions are higher up in the chain of command, where they tend to be furthest from the nitty-gritty. I worked on an extensive program where people were deployed at team, programme or leadership levels. The team, programme and leadership coaches were permitted (and most likely bound by contract) to work only at their designated level. When they offered their help at another level, they were shut down. Speaking up for oneself was prohibited. To sum it up, within this hierarchy, the chain of command was so segregated that no one had a holistic idea of what was going on. This created a situation that's commonly referred to as watermelon syndrome.

A watermelon is green on the outside and red on the inside. The people who are closely involved with a project's development are inside the watermelon, so to speak. In this project they were aware of the issues, so to them everything looks red. Those in leadership positions were standing outside the watermelon and viewing it externally as a whole, so from where they were standing, the watermelon looked green. The project appeared to be going perfectly well. They talked only with the stakeholders, who were viewing the project from the same perspective.

Those who were directly involved in the project (including software developers, testers, business analysts and the like) had the red view, so they reported that the problems were huge and needed to be immediately addressed. Those who were further away, with the green view, shrugged them off as simply being complainers. *Relax*, they said. *Things can't always be perfect.*

It's very difficult for me to convince the leadership to address pressing issues that they view as being peripheral. By preventing me from making the necessary systemic changes, they preserve the very structure that stands in the way of the company's progress. In this way, I'm coerced into upholding the very structure that I was hired to overhaul. That's why, in many companies, the hierarchy and the status quo remain unchanged.

WHAT TO CONSIDER OR TRY NOW

- **Report** on fact-based metrics based on objective mile-stones. Present metrics that have a visible evidence and therefore no one can hide from. Ideally present something tangible, something already (partially) working to create visible impressions. Better than percentage of documentation complete, use percentage of feature functionality tested and experienceable.

- **Consider** metrics from three different areas: progress metrics (towards the objectives), product/service metrics (reporting on the quality of what you offer or produce) and process metrics (how efficiently you're working or how you improve the way you work).

HIRING EXTERNALS AS NEW INTERNALS SHOULD DO THE TRICK.

As will be discussed in greater detail in a forthcoming chapter, organisations compete for the best talent. Hiring excellent personnel is vital to a company's success. When someone who has worked with the company as an external proves to be an asset, the company may decide to directly hire this person. Why should this person choose to work with the company in question? Likely incentives include: a competitive salary, the opportunity to travel less for work, and the potential for career advancement.

Coming back to the example of the football teams, in such a competitive sport, immediate results are of critical importance. As the success of a team is what attracts commercial partners, the team's current dominance of the sport takes priority over the long-term development goal. If you look at the players for whom teams are willing to pay the highest fees, there is a general trend towards securing mature players who can provide some guarantee of instant success, rather than developing emerging talent or mid-career players and developing them over time. It is difficult to predict how long it takes to develop a player and the outcome is not certain. As the saying goes, it is not a war for talent but a need for skills.

I have observed quite a few organisations who hire directly from their suppliers. While this is not a bad tactic in and of itself, I wonder whether these companies are relying too heavily on it. In football terms, they are banking on the mature players and greying out the area in which they need to develop themselves, of growing talent. They should strive to create a unique selling proposition to attract and retain employees. They should be recruiting the future stars of tomorrow and growing together with them, even if it means they don't win the championship every year, so to speak.

WHAT TO CONSIDER OR TRY NOW

- **When** hiring, think about modern ways to market and process the job offer.

  ☑ Phrase job ads in an inclusive style

  ☑ Consolidate the essential information about your target group

  ☑ Analyse data and channels with analytics tools

  ☑ Use and promote employee referrals

  ☑ Use virtual reality (VR) to give your remote candidates a realistic tour of your office location and show applicants your company culture

  ☑ Switch things up with your interview locations and questions—no more standard office meetings and questions such as "Where do you see yourself in three years?"

- **If you're** the one applying for a job, be different and make yourself stand out. Familiarise yourself with the competition and come up with creative ways to sell yourself to your targeted employer.

THERE'S NO TIME TO LEARN AND IMPROVE; THE PROBLEMS WE HAVE, MUST BE DEALT WITH IMMEDIATELY.

Companies are always in a rush to get things done. Almost invariably, they are behind with the product, the idea, the invention, the timeline. They'll throw a bunch of people (usually including external consultants) at the problem: *Just get it done—we can always improve it later.* Whether the mission is to deliver a project, launch a product or conduct a training course, let's bring on board as many people as we can and complete it in the shortest possible time span.

This approach effectively rules out the possibility of personnel development or continuing education of talent. When you simply throw money and people at a problem and do whatever it takes to get the job done, quality is typically not an important part of the equation. This is a false economy, because taking shortcuts will compromise the quality of the work and create issues that will eventually resurface and will eat up all the money that was saved.

Developers are artists, not factory workers. Nor are they machines that simply require occasional maintenance.

Even if it's clear that a company has been doing something wrong for years, and that this is the reason why the teams are falling behind schedule, the familiar mantra comes out. There's no time for reform, as we need to deliver now. *Next time, we'll do everything right.* This promise is rarely fulfilled, because time is always scarce, demand is always high, and people are always busy. Hasn't that been the case for the last decades?

WHAT TO CONSIDER OR TRY NOW

- **Before** scaling up, assemble a tiger team. A tiger team is a group of specialists from a range of specific fields who work together on a mission. Appoint an interdisciplinary team of experts to lay the groundwork and initial structures. People joining afterward can build upon this framework, so that a high-level order is given which prevents chaos and inefficiency of too many people being thrown at a common task too early.

- **Never** jump to a temporary measure to which you would not be prepared to commit as long-term. As the Russian proverb goes: "Nothing is more permanent than a temporary solution."

07 | HIDDEN AGENDA

S O MUCH ENERGY BECOMES DIVERTED INTO CALCULATING, MA-noeuvring and negotiating the politics involved in everyday business life. At the majority of companies with whom I have worked, I've observed how political intrigue pulses underneath every interaction. Everyone is looking out for their own best interests, often at the expense of others in the team and in the company. Their self-serving strategy is not aligned with the objectives of their teams or of the company, and it is an exploitation of the company's resources. They are taking as much as they can squeeze out of the company. It is not necessarily a bad thing to follow a personal development plan, but to execute it with this level of focus strikes me as somewhat chilling.

> When you become bored at work, it is time to adjust your mindset. Entrepreneurial spirit should drive every employee.

Let's say you've just started fresh at a new company. You may have joined the company because you were impressed by the people you met during the interview process, because you like the company's products or because you believe in its vision of the future. You should have two goals in mind:

- to further your personal development
- to make the company more successful

Joining a company is always something special. You get to know your colleagues, find your place in the company, come to understand how work is carried out, and learn how to deal with the internal processes. You bond with your colleagues. Together you overcome obstacles and setbacks and celebrate successes. After some time, you begin to realise and appreciate where you are. Your mindset starts to shift. Instead of simply pursuing your personal ambitions, you're working towards the shared success of your team or your company. You ask yourself: *How can I help the company to be more successful?* Eventually, this develops into: *How can I help ensure the company's success in the future?* At some point, something shifts the focus from your own wellbeing to the company's success. After a while, the company's course becomes your course. You would defend the company. You stand for what it stands for. When the company succeeds, you succeed.

This is the best-case scenario and something we all should have in mind when joining a new company or project. However, all too often, things turn out differently. Every achievement and goal become entangled in a web of politics. Loyalty and teamwork go out the window, and success is only measured in terms of personal gain. The company ends up having to carry its employees. If it doesn't, people will abandon ship. While the stories I'm about to share with you may sound extreme, I'm sad to report that I've observed many work environments that resemble these cases.

UNLESS THE PROJECT IS A PERFECT MATCH FOR ME, I'LL LEAVE.

I worked on a project with one company whose employees weren't happy with a particular set of circumstances. As some of them seemed to believe they were powerless to change the situation, instead of attempting to negotiate matters, they behaved in a very compromising way. One individual declared: *If we are really going to proceed in this manner, I will leave the company. I need to work within the original setup that was in place when I started working here. Otherwise, I won't commit.*

I was surprised, to say the least. I wondered whether the person was simply trying to make a splash. I had to wonder how this person's colleagues felt. They must have wondered: *Which line have we crossed to make someone speak of quitting? Is this the work environment for which we strive?*

What if such a thing were to happen in our personal lives? Would a friend walk away in the middle of a conversation because they don't agree with something you've said? You'd talk things over. One of you might come around to the other person's point of view or you might agree to disagree. Either way, it wouldn't be the end of the friendship. It all comes down to a question of respect. If you respect someone, you'll respect their point of view, even when it differs from yours.

This was a systemic issue as well as a personal one. True, the company structure needed to change, but this individual lacked the compassion, dedication and drive to change their current environment.

We have witnessed similar behaviour in the last couple of years in politics. While setting boundaries is a sign of integrity, issuing ultimatums is an act of desperation. You are giving up the fight and ruling out the possibility of coming to a compromise through further discussion. As well as revealing a lack of creativity, adaptability and entrepreneurial spirit, it signals that you have no interest in working together toward a solution or being part of a team.

Of course, there are times when enough is enough. Ultimatums have their place, but they should be a last resort. In the feature film

Live From Baghdad, Michael Keaton plays the CNN reporter Anthony Wiener, who remained in Iraq long after all the other journalists had left. He says that *as soon as the countries stop talking to each other, the war will begin.*

WHAT TO CONSIDER OR TRY NOW

- **Listen** to what people are saying. Try to find out what has changed (or is currently changing) that has so adversely affected the outlook. Perhaps the preceding situation was simply too good to be true, and people got used to it. There is at least a grain of truth in everything you hear. Apply discernment but do not disregard anyone outright, especially not those who are outspoken. These people may be voicing what others think but don't dare to say. Based upon what you have learned, create alliances and tackle the situation to change it for the better.

- **It may** be helpful to learn about the various emotional stages that may emerge during this time. The Kübler-Ross model of the stages of grief[75] is applicable to any period of major change. The five stages are: denial, anger, bargaining, depression, acceptance. Being able to recognise which stage an individual is currently experiencing can help you to choose the appropriate response and modes of interaction.

- **You** may find yourself dealing with someone who is resigned and despondent or someone with the highest expectations. Conduct a quick reality check. Are their impressions based on facts or emotions? Either way, your first step is to engage in a conversation on the reasons. If you are not able to have an open and constructive dialogue or derive actions, it may be time to escalate the matter to a supervisor or line manager.

---

[75] Crowther, Linnea. "The Five Stages of Grief." 19 February 2019. Legacy.com. https://legcy.co/2DNO2rr

DO NOT DESTROY OUR PROJECT; IT IS A CONSTANT SOURCE OF REVENUE.

I was involved with one project that reminded me of a Paul Auster novel called *The Book of Illusions*, in that it eventually trapped us inside a reality encased within other realities.

A company wanted to migrate their product portfolio to state-of-the-art technology, including optimised processes. It started small, with a few migration parts, as well as a couple of areas that needed to be built entirely from scratch. The project grew increasingly larger and more unwieldy. As it grew, it sucked in more labour, time, and budget. It was a black hole. A release date was set, and the hype machine was set in motion. As you might have already guessed, it failed spectacularly and had to be written off—on paper, that is. The project itself endured.

What was to be done with this half-baked pie? It contained all the necessary ingredients—the right people and software—but was a gloppy mess. In the second act, rather than throwing it out, the company hatched a new plan. *We have already spent all this money. We're almost halfway there.* Where have we heard this before?

The company appointed a new project manager, installed new control structures, and created a more detailed and rigorous plan. The teams formulated a programme and set up numerous projects within that programme to help govern it. These projects were expected to help them deliver results in a more appropriate, timely, autonomous and streamlined manner. What happened instead was that these projects became increasingly opaque.

Politics, influence, and dependencies had to be nurtured, even as deadlines loomed and the scope of the project continued to grow. The release date was postponed more than once, and a greater number of people was brought on board. In the meantime, certain people had shifted into very powerful positions, and parts of the program were progressing rather well. External suppliers began to compete among themselves in an effort to prove themselves to be their client's most willing, capable and reliable partner. Unfortunately, dependencies between the projects and a common release plan contravened these actions.

Had they seized this opportunity to learn from each other, they might have made this program the company's forerunner for the 21st century. They should have incorporated decoupled architecture, incremental development and on-demand deployment, run A/B tests and discovery phases with specific customer groups. They should have introduced new functionality and run tests with focus groups. Instead of experimenting and innovating, they focused on making minor changes somewhere within the product. It took weeks to figure out that, given the consequences, dependencies on other areas, and an overarching reluctance to change anything at all, it was simply too risky.

In the third act, the company decided to implement a new modus operandi within parts of this project, to increase flexibility, safeguard against failure, generate more experiments, accelerate speed to market, and establish a technical support system so that people feel more involved and empowered to speak up and run experiments.

This is the moment when I encountered the following sentence which would ring in my ears for weeks afterwards: *We approve of your projection of the future, but do not risk the project.* This effectively wiped out any hopes of a renaissance for the company, as it revealed a mindset of: *Although we're willing to try out a new project management style, on the whole, we'll do everything the way we've been doing it for the last few years.*

Following several failed attempts to find common ground, navigate a way forward, and socialise the topic to become more in novative, independent and flexible, the company discontinued the improvement initiative. This decision was taken primarily because it had come to light that the company was currently operating approximately fifty-seven initiatives (including technical, hiring, re-organisation, decommissioning, downsizing, migration, and up-grading initiatives). Their reasoning went something like this: *We have lost the overview of our spending, and our portfolio of actions lacks transparency. Therefore, we must stop everything except for a few key initiatives.* Take a wild guess at which program survived.

Many valuable and productive initiatives were discontinued. Most of the people employed on these projects were external contractors, who either left the company or were delegated to other tasks and projects. Of these, the only project that was not closed down is the colossal programme, along with its menagerie of projects, which had caused spending to spiral out of control.

At the time of writing, it is still running (and, I'm guessing, still consuming everything in its path). I have no doubt that there will be more chapters in the story with every dawning realisation of what can be accomplished, *if only we did this or that.* The question is, for how long this continue? Will the tides ever turn?

What can we learn from this experience? Even though a lot of effort had been invested in this project, it shouldn't have been so hard to kill. The other scenario to be avoided is the way the pendulum swung back and forth between two extremes. At one end, we had a self-organised, laissez-faire approach; and at the other, very rigid structure and micromanagement.

WHAT TO CONSIDER OR TRY NOW

- **Any** programme should be started with a clear vision in mind. Test it out or simulate it via a fast-forward workshop: Close your eyes and have someone else guide your thought process while hearing about a future time and form in which the vision took shape. Questions to consider include: *How do you feel then? What do people say about you? How is your day going? What does the press say?* Explore the situation in a playful and reflective way.

- **Start small,** and prove your vision. Big programmes tend to be inefficient. Start small, keeping investments limited and focused. Prove your results before you begin, via hypotheses and measurements. Ask yourself: what is the smallest thing (sometimes called minimal viable feature - MVF). I can build that is sufficient to convince others and demonstrates a piece of what we're going to build?

- **Find** an active sponsor, who is as high up in your organisation as possible, to support your vision and minimise political plays.

- **Create** the future in small but consistent intermediate steps. This allows everyone to get accustomed to the new normal. Create successes with this new stable situation to convince the cynics. Then start a new small step forward.

BEING A SUPERHERO HAS ONLY ADVANTAGES.

The person who said this to me was Susanne, the bona fide superhero, who simultaneously occupied the roles of software developer, product manager and team lead. (This scenario took place in an Agile setup and concerned these roles but could apply to any constellation of roles.)

One could argue that it makes sense, as long as it is not too much work for one person, as keeping it lean means decision making is quicker, teams are smaller, and fewer misunderstandings are likely to occur. Susanne followed up with: *Anyway, it's best that all of these duties are performed by one person. This way, it is clear who decides what, and I don't need to hold any time-consuming meetings with others to align or hand things over. All the information and expertise are contained within one person.*

It is not necessarily a bad thing to keep things as lean as possible. However, she then went on to say that monopolising these responsibilities ensured that she wouldn't get the sack if things were to go wrong. First, because Susanne was undoubtedly crucial to the project, no one would ever question her authority. Second, the fact that she was doing all three jobs at once would provide a viable excuse for not doing any of these jobs correctly.

I was floored, to say the least. Fair play. Future secured. Susanne expressed such blatant disregard for what the outcome might be for the company. In her world, the priority is simply to make sure that no one threatens her position.

WHAT TO CONSIDER OR TRY NOW

- **Work out** the truck factor[76] of your project. If your truck factor is low, this may indicate that you have head monopolies. Similar to having superheroes, this renders you vulnerable as you are too dependent upon too few persons. If any of these persons were to exit the company or take a long sick leave or vacation, it will cause a bottleneck.

- **See** also Chapter 03. Question of Time, story "I am doing three jobs in parallel..." where we elaborate on how to handle superheros

---

[76] Bowler, Michael. "Truck Factor." 15 May 2005. https://bit.ly/31VYcOp

MY ROLE IS INDISPENSABLE.

Years ago, I met Craig Larman, who introduced a new way of working in the company I was working for at that time. He is a very controversial character and is not shy of being brutally direct. While addressing approximately 250 company employees and their CEO, Larman said:

> [Y]ou have a choice to make, and this will define your future career. There are three options that I will draft for you. You will be the best engineer, with technical skills galore. Or, you will become the best product manager, and drive this company towards new heights in terms of innovative, customer-centric products. Or, you will become an agent for change and foster a new way of working, act as a catalyst and strive towards continuous improvement. To all middle managers, dependency managers, release managers, thank you for your service. If you want to remain in these positions, this company is not for you anymore. There's job safety, but no role safety.[77]

Larman's speech made a lasting impression on everyone present that day. The traditional career model still applies in so many companies. A typical path starts with being a great technician, becoming the tech or team lead, then taking over departments and moving into management. At some point, you come to a fork in the road. You can't simultaneously lead technical teams and do technical stuff, as your time is consumed by jours fixes, financial calculations, team meetings, vendor selections, and contract negotiations. If you're also still trying to cling to technical aspects, things will get complicated. And yet, line organisational duties pave the way to promotion. That's how it works within most companies.

[77] "Introduction to Large-Scale Scrum (LeSS)." Craig Larman. YouTube (video). Accessed 24 July 2020. https://bit.ly/343L9gw

As your company moves towards a more reliable project organisation, you'll have to decide which hat you are going to wear. Will you be in charge of line organisation, assigning work and deciding upon priorities? These work items will decrease over time, since the majority of work (and, most likely, the most exciting work) lies in project assignments. However, these will already have a project manager or product owner (someone with exquisite knowledge about the product and project) in place. Is the project manager the same as the person in charge of line organisation? Will you be redundant? Or will you cling to your responsibilities, even if it complicates matters within the company? How far will you go to try to keep matters in your own hands? Would you go so far as to block the opportunity to get things done?

WHAT TO CONSIDER OR TRY NOW

- Get familiar with Agile methods, roles and careers. The different types of leadership respectively management roles are divided into three primary domains: business/product, IT/architecture, methods/processes. All roles from these three domains scale up from the typical instances you would find within teams (e.g., developer to senior developer, architect to enterprise architect) all the way to overarching roles. As all of these remain content driven across several levels within the hierarchy, the balance between the management and expert track tilts toward the content-driven expert careers, with the exception of pure management roles. This is well suited to the time of the knowledge worker, when knowledge, including competence or skills, makes all the difference. See also Chapter 6. Culture Eats Strategy For Breakfast and story This Does Not Match My Job Description for information on more modern role descriptions.

- **Read up** on how new models such as network-centric organisations[78] are increasingly replacing hierarchies as the primary structure[79] and driving companies towards more value-driven or customer-oriented structures. They base upon a set of teams that are not connected by a hierarchy but by customer needs and dependencies. You probably won't see this scale up to one large system having hundreds of teams. The trend we see with the pioneers out there, e.g. Morning Star Company[80] and Handelsbanken is to limit the team of teams structure to 150-400 people.

- **Getting** rid of management stresses the need for leadership and extended personal processes (e.g., coaching of employees). This, however, is transferred to people managers/leads and similar roles or remains the primary task of the still-existing line organisation. While these are secondary to network or value stream-based organisations, they still have their place. Change management guru John Kotter calls this co-existence a dual operating system.[81]

---

[78] "Network-centric organization." Wikipedia. Last modified 30 April 2020. https://bit.ly/3g1x45A

[79] Pflaeging, Niels. "Agile Is Beta—keynote by Niels Pflaeging at Comelion 2019." LinkedIn SlideShare. Accessed 24 July 2020. https://bit.ly/3kMxbpf

[80] Hamel, Gary. "First, Let's Fire All the Managers." *Harvard Business Review.* From the Dec. 2011 issue. https://bit.ly/3kEMxeJ

[81] Kotter, John P. "Accelerate!" *Harvard Business Review.* Nov. 2012 issue. https://hbr.org/2012/11/accelerate

WHENEVER THERE IS TOO MUCH WORK, I DELEGATE; PROBLEM SOLVED.

Let's say an organisation has started to take on more projects, each of which is assigned a fixed delivery date from the outset, but it does not increase its workforce. How will it manage to cope with all of these projects? It doesn't. So, what does it do? It appoints more managers to manage the plans, in the belief that more coordination in multi-tasking will increase efficiency and speed up delivery. The organisation's leadership assumes that the people who build the products are to blame—that they are not fulfilling their potential because they are lazy.

"Knowledge workers must know more about their job than their boss does."

—Peter Drucker

It is not as simple as bringing in another person to get the job done—it's a question of who's responsible. Therefore, this is not about the engineers who carry out the technical work but about the management side. There are simply not enough people to be distributed to projects when only project demand increases but the workforce remains stable. One more project would be one project too many. Bringing in another manager to cover for them leads to more complexity and splits the existing work between even more people, which leads to more handover and less transparency. Taking this action undermines their authority. The intention is good—they want to appoint someone else to take over the day-to-day work. Yet it shouldn't require this much coordination.

There were too many things being pushed towards these people as it was, and, due to career advancement or not being able to say *No*, they will eventually end up doing all of it anyway. It becomes a vicious cycle. Instead of hiring more employees to carry out the actual engineering delivery or simply turning down some projects until they can get on top of things, the leadership introduces more coordination more jour fixes. Meetings become incredibly protracted affairs. This is compounded by the managers' weakness (whether actual or perceived). Personal self-advancement is prioritised above successful project delivery. Thus, the option of turning down projects is never even considered.

Instead of bringing in more delegates, which serves only to complicate matters further, companies might do well to go back to the basics. In 1903, an American mechanical engineer called Frederick Winslow Taylor wrote his seminal paper *Shop Management*, in which he emphasised the labour component of manufacturing and quantified it in terms of *product rates per hour*. Taylor sought to improve industrial efficiency and was one of the first management consultants. He said that in the past, man had come first, but in the future, systems would come first. He proposed a method called scientific management, which operated on the four main principles that I've paraphrased below.

1 | **Use scientific methods to study work and determine the most efficient way to perform specific tasks.** Don't just work by "rule of thumb," simple habit and common sense. This is misleading and doesn't help keeping the focus.

2 | **Match workers to jobs based on their capability and motivation.** Don't just arbitrarily assigning workers to jobs, and train them to work at maximum efficiency.

3 | **Provide instructions and supervision to ensure that they're using the most efficient ways of working.** This is being done by monitoring performance.

4 | **Managers spend their time planning and training, allowing workers to perform their tasks efficiently.** This way work between managers and workers are allocated.[82]

---

[82] "Frederick Taylor and Scientific Management: Understanding Taylorism and Early Management Theory." *Mind Tools* (website). Accessed 28 June 2020. https://bit.ly/3cm4RX2

Clearly, there are more holistic ways to look at the workplace. Other experts have refined and developed Taylor's work in the intervening years, and we now know that frameworks and working principles work when they are adopted in their entirety and when the system surrounding the framework is right as well.

While it's easy to pick holes in theories that were set out years ago, it seems more helpful to acknowledge them as a foundation upon which we are free to build. The strategies he recommended—systematic selection and training procedures, studying workplace efficiency, and systematic organisational design—are not so far from what we would consider to be great organisational design and a viable system for intrinsic motivation of employees.

WHAT TO CONSIDER OR TRY NOW

Modern thinking on project management finds its roots in the work of Frederick Taylor. We moved from the industrial period into the digital and knowledge-oriented era. More people work with their minds than perform physical labour. For this type of work, in the current economy, people management needs re-thinking. While the idea of training and measuring progress remains quite stable, some new trends fly in.

- **Let** people pull work toward them, instead of pushing work toward them. In other words, avoid command-and-control styles of management.

- **Lead** people instead of managing them. There are many references drawing the distinction between leaders and managers. While the importance of leadership grows, you'll still need both competencies. There is no one right way to lead people.

- **Do not** micromanage. Instead, apply intent-based leadership.[83] Set the target and let people find their own way. Naturally, you'll still want to ensure that you provide the relevant training and support.

- **Eliminate** the two-tier system between managers and workers. Instead, each has their own area of competence, in which they can take decisions autonomously.

---

[83] "David Marquet: Intent-Based Leadership." The ArmyLeader.co.uk. Accessed 27 July 2020. https://bit.ly/3at9IoD

I AM DOING THIS TASK SIMPLY OUT OF COURTESY TO MY BOSS.

This statement is unsettling for anyone who believes that people all possess the entrepreneurial spirit and strive towards success in terms of building successful companies. One could argue that people need to be within the right environment or system to prosper and feel appreciated, therefore bringing out their best. I accept that not everyone has their dream job or the freedom to prosper. Still, shouldn't we embrace the life we have?

Years ago, at a seminar I attended, I heard the story of John Christensen, the owner of *ChartHouse Learning*. In 1997, he visited Seattle's Pike Place Fish Market, where he saw fishmongers tossing salmon and trout in the air. This dynamic display engaged and entertained onlookers and helped with sales. Christensen was impressed by how the fishmongers had transformed a job that could have been rather mundane into something everyone could enjoy, simply by doing it with enthusiasm and a sense of fun. Christensen interviewed and filmed the fishmongers and ended up creating the *Fish Philosophy*, which can be summarised in the key principles listed below.

> **You have power over how you feel at work.**

- Be emotionally present for people
- Play, be creative and enthusiastic, and have fun
- Make people's day in a meaningful, memorable way
- Choose your attitude

The whole seminar was structured around this topic and it really struck a chord with me. Since then I try to be present and make the best of every situation. Making the best of a situation means something different to everyone. For some people, it means doing whatever it takes to advance their own position. Helping other might be further down their list of priorities. At one company, I was supposed to work with one of its managers on a few challenging topics regarding change management, leadership, and enforcing certain practices on some people who were not highly motivated. He asked me for help, which was a good start. After that, he did very little, and I became the go-to guy. That was his answer to the problem. Problem solved.

He was there because his boss had asked him to be. He was not motivated to do anything more than the bare minimum. Why should he? He saw no benefit in investing any of his energy into these tasks. He said that he didn't know what was happening, he didn't understand the topic, he didn't like the people involved, and he had way too many overtime hours, which he wasn't willing to give up.

Instead of going on vacation, he had jumped at the chance to pitch in and help his boss, so that he could keep his overtime hours. He wanted to spend his time without expending any extra effort—just following his normal routine, which consisted of reading, smoking, chatting to other people in person and on the phone, and having long lunch breaks.

This served to clear up some of the mystery surrounding why some people are so hard to work with. Their motivation lies somewhere else entirely: *The salary stream is steady, so let me focus on my personal life.* During working hours, of course.

WHAT TO CONSIDER OR TRY NOW

■ **When** dealing with an employee who is flying below the radar, here are some considerations and strategies to help you assess and address the situation.

☑ An employee who is content to carry out the job description to the letter—nothing less and nothing more—won't change the world but is actually not causing an immediate problem. Even if this person's performance is regarded by others as mediocre, lacklustre or too rigidly focused, is it in fact satisfactory or is there a specific cause for concern? If it is the latter, you'll want to attend to it sooner rather than later.

☑ Unless there are extenuating factors that can be changed, you may consider moving the person to an environment that's better suited to their skills and personal strengths. As facilitating such a transition is time-consuming for all parties involved, organisations will generally view this as a last resort and are likely to take other measures first.

☑ Ascertain whether this runs deeper than an attitude problem. If the person's performance is being compromised by a skills deficit or a health condition, things are unlikely to improve without their seeking external help.

☑ Is this person unwilling to change or is he not allowed to perform in any other way? It's essential to understand all of the moving parts. How does the system allow this person to interact with all of the surrounding players and variables? The issue may be with a supervisor, a peer or the organisation's rules or restrictions.

I'M HAPPY TO HELP OTHER PEOPLE OUT, BUT DON'T HOLD ME ACCOUNTABLE IF THINGS GO WRONG.

Are responsibility and accountability interchangeable terms? We tend to speak of responsibility when a project is going well; and accountability seems to rear its head only when things are going badly. Responsibility defines one's duties and actions to be taken; accountability centres on reporting to others and assigning blame.

As I have mentioned, I have often observed situations in which people try to make someone else the scapegoat for everything that has gone wrong with a project. No one is willing to accept the blame.

"Come yourself or send no one."

—W. Edwards Deming

People say: *The structures have not been made clear enough. I should have been better informed.* Just for once, I would like to see teams pulling together instead of assigning blame. We are all in this together.

If I help someone, I must also take ownership of my actions. Once involved with a cause, I will support it to the best of my ability. Once I contribute to a project, I am automatically responsible. If you realise the task is something you will not be able to do, you had better say so and give the other person the chance to react. If you say nothing, because you don't feel any responsibility to speak up, the result will be worse than if you had never gotten involved.

I often hear statements such as: *I have stepped in for the time being, but I don't know the details.* Or: *I can decide this or that, but I will be here just as long as my colleague is on leave. Please do not expect me to answer all of your questions. I am here just to keep the lights on and act as an authority.* That last sentence makes me laugh. People will find out, sooner than later, that the stand-in neither has any authority nor is someone they can rely on. This substitute only stands in the way of progress, making things more complicated or blocking decisions. Things just get worse every time the responsibility is shifted to someone else. In the long run, the responsibility ends up somewhere in the void, and a vacuum is created. The stand-in's poor performance also undermines the credibility of the real authority figure, as they were the one who appointed the deputy.

WHAT TO CONSIDER OR TRY NOW

- **In project** management, especially when mobilising projects and defining the rules of the game, we define RACI matrices. The four capital letters in RACI stand for responsible, accountable, consulted and informed. Together they define the degree of involvement and influence each role has on certain topics and tasks within the project.

- **Here** are a few steps to help you delegate more effectively:

  - ☑ Understand when to delegate and when not to

  - ☑ Be clear about your target and communicate it clearly to others

  - ☑ Appoint a person who has enough available time and the relevant expertise and skills

  - ☑ Trust but verify—agree upon deadlines, including feedback loops

  - ☑ Get buy-in; don't push

  - ☑ Set clear guardrails (minimum acceptance criteria) for the one taking over

  - ☑ Offer support as needed, making clear that it is fully acceptable to ask for it (and unacceptable to intentionally bypass it)

  - ☑ Upon completion, show your appreciation

■ **When** you allocate a task, you are instructing a subordinate to carry it out; you tell them what to do and they do it without complaint: This is a behaviour which stems from command & control management. It is also called a Push behaviour instead of Pull. In Pull mode subordinates would choose what to do out of a given set of prioritized tasks. Delegation involves transferring some of your own work to another person. Rather than simply following a set of instructions, they take over a role that requires them to make decisions and be held accountable for the outcomes. The previous mentioned approach on Intent-based / Intentional Leadership[84] fits to this.

---

[84] "David Marquet: Intent-Based Leadership." The ArmyLeader.co.uk. Accessed 27 July 2020. https://bit.ly/3at9IoD

08 | GROW UNTIL YOU CAN'T FAIL ANYMORE

OMPANIES STRIVE FOR GROWTH. THEY HIRE MORE EMPLOYEES so they can earn more revenue, exert more influence, and dominate a greater segment of the market. Everywhere you look, in sports and in business, the numbers are going up. In this hyper-connected society, human interaction is crucial.

Even though automation and self-service enable us to achieve more at a faster pace with minimum human intervention, we will never negate the need for human interaction. Closing a business deal requires a modicum of trust. People need to talk with each other face to face. We can communicate in real time with people on the other side of the world via telephone and video conferencing, yet business travel, whether by ground or air, continues steadily increasing. Clearly, we need to see, touch and feel the products and industry buildings in which we trade or invest and meet the people with whom we conduct our business.

In the business world, especially when we feel as if we're drowning in messages, files and notifications, it can be tempting to check out mentally and to hide behind the technology. The human element gets lost, and we begin to disappear. We have the power to reverse this trend. Instead of being so focused on networking, with the purpose of increasing our range of connections, we might strive to have more meaningful conversations and encounters. To really make a difference, quality is more important than quantity. It's about deepening your connection with people rather than widening your circle.

Never underestimate the power of direct human interaction, even in the digital world.

Instead of simply being in contact, why not try to really connect? The next time you write an e-mail or make a call, instead of rattling off the usual string of pleasantries and clichés, why not take a moment to picture the person at the other end and think of something genuine to say to them? I consciously try to make my social interactions mindful and meaningful and to make them count. Our lives are so much more fulfilling and enjoyable when we genuinely communicate and engage with each other.

Let's take a look at some of the soul-destroying habits we encounter on a near-daily basis.

I WILL DO ANYTHING TO DEFEND MY POSITION IN THE COMPANY.

The higher up people are in the company's hierarchy, the more responsibility and power of influence they have. They often use this power to protect themselves and their cronies. It is a well-known pattern. We see people ending up in positions without having a clue about what is expected of them. They may not even be qualified to take on the task. Why are so many organisations structured this way? Harvard Business Review's blog Ascend recently published an article that argues that the vertical structure of companies reflects the belief that our careers are vertical and that corporate environments operate through the process of elimination. It goes on to say:

> [T]oday's work is no longer divided up into small tasks that require higher and higher layers of management to put together. Instead most work is accomplished through horizontal processes that cut across different functions, geographies, and specialties. Therefore, real success comes less from controlling people that report to you, and more from the ability to align stakeholders who surround you.[85]

We have been aware for some time that hierarchical structures have little relevance to the way businesses actually operate nowadays. There needs to be a new career model. Some companies or, in some cases, the individual departments within them, are too slow to respond to changes in the economy. While those in leadership positions have the power to dismantle these structures, they are the ones who have scaled these hierarchies and given an arm and a leg to ensconce themselves within the upper echelons. It is in their best interests to protect the status quo, as they don't know where they will stand within the new pecking order. Who can really blame them?

A person we'll call Amber wants to work for a particular company. Amber goes through the interview process and manages to secure a position.

Amber Ambitious - the new star on the horizon.
She learns fast. Motivated and self-driven.
A successful career lies ahead of her.

Particularly during the first months at this new job, she has to prove herself. Finally, she settles in. She starts to work her way up

[85] Ashkenas, Ron. "Your Career Needs to Be Horizontal." *Ascend* (blog). *Harvard Business Review.* 7 July 2019. https://hbrascend.org/topics/career-needs-horizontal/

in the company. Eventually, she proves her value and establishes herself as a respected member of the team.

A few years pass. Amber's ascent seems to have plateaued. She notes that the company is flooded with new hires, some of whom could be seen to be in direct competition with her. Amber fears that she will be overlooked when the question of promotion comes up.

The company's structure is traditional, therefore hierarchical. You have the teams headed by team leads; then the departments headed by department leads; and then the business areas headed by business area leads. Some management areas are free floating, including project management, quality, testing, and other governance teams such as security. At the top, you have upper management, who lead across some of the areas mentioned above. Above them, leadership, also known as C-level personnel.

Hierarchies stall companies.

Moving up means acquiring greater responsibility. Amber believes she has the opportunity and domain knowledge to progress into middle management and beyond. As long as the new hires haven't found their bearings or fully settled in, Amber feels that she's managing to stay a few steps ahead. At this stage, she has two options. She can prove her value by doing mentoring work, helping others, and learning from others, to remain in a strong position on the team and add to creating the best results for the team, and, ultimately, for the company. Or, she may attempt to climb the company ladder by putting in her bid to become a team lead.

The latter option is the more challenging of the two, as she will have to put everything on the line and prove her worth to upper management. In this company, this requires considerable skill in political manoeuvres, arguing, and deflecting responsibility and blame. Anyone who sets out on this path must be prepared to stake everything on it. It's a one-way ticket to the end of the line.

Nepotism is a strong word—let's just say that it's no secret that ambitious people tend to forge close connections on their way up and, once in the seat of power, they protect those networks to the extent that they create counterintuitive dependencies and introduce extra layers of complexity. Once they sit in those corner offices, they certainly will honour those loyalties, as well as benefiting from them. Whether or not they are actually capable of dealing with the challenges and duties required of them, no one will ever know, as at this level and in such a hierarchical setting, politics and intrigues are more important than technical or business skills.

Therefore, Amber essentially has the choice to remain a slave to the system, striving only to protect and advance her position, or she can seek to change the system for the better.

WHAT TO CONSIDER OR TRY NOW

- **Check in** with a friend or someone in the position you're targeting. Ask them whether they can imagine you in this position. Ask them questions that will help you to better understand the requirements, permissions and responsibilities involved.

- **Find out** if your company uses Agile management methods. If so, the path to promotion may be less political and more merit-driven than in traditional organisations.

- **If you** are looking to assume more responsibility, consider gaining more experience in content-based leadership, e.g., getting someone ready to take over your role or leading two or three people in small (temporary) projects. Try it out and learn from the experience.

- **Circle** back to some of the ideas we have been exploring throughout the book and work on these areas. Think about what motivates you. Find your ikigai (see **Chapter 6. Culture Eats Strategy for Breakfast**) and shape your life accordingly. Set some new objectives that might be different from simply a career growth step toward more management and accountability.

- **Based** on the work of Frederic Laloux[86], above all, our culture values profit and growth, and beating the competition. If you find yourself in today's typical corporations the career paths are built along this mindset.

[86] Laloux, Frederic. Reinventing Organizations: a Guide to Creating Organizations. Inspired by the next Stage of Human Consciousness. Brussels: Nelson Parker, 2014.

THE MORE PEOPLE I HAVE WORKING FOR ME, THE MORE RELEVANCE I HAVE.

This archaic mode of thinking remains deeply entrenched. In a world that is ever moving towards team efforts and collaboration, it is surprising that people still equate influence, clout and relevance so heavily with the number of people who report to them. I can appreciate that having a great number of people working under you might make you feel more valued, because they will view you as a mentor. It may slightly increase your sphere of influence, as they may be less likely to backstab you and more likely to put in a good word for you. All of these things help to cement your foothold within the company. Any good work they do will reflect well upon you.

Decisions should be taken where the competency is.

However, when companies make changes to improve their time-to-market and speed of decision making as is inevitable, things tend to shift in favour of more direct decision making. People will want to step up and take matters in their own hands. In some cases things will become so complicated that it is no longer possible for a single person to oversee the whole construct. This knife cuts both ways. A 2017 article from McKinsey states:

> [L]eaders are less able to delegate decisions cleanly, and the number of decision-makers has risen. The reduced cost of communications brought on by the digital age has compounded matters by bringing more people into the flow via email.[87]

Generally speaking, decisions should be moved to where they can actually be best taken.

---

[87] De Smet, Aaron, Gerald Lackey, Leigh M. Weiss. "Untangling Your Organization's Decision Making." 17 June 2017. *McKinsey Quarterly.* McKinsey & Company.

WHAT TO CONSIDER OR TRY NOW

- **Due to** the change in careers and career paths due to the different nature of work and economy in the 21st century, organisations are becoming flattened, and management and leadership are defined in a new way. As things move in this direction, traditional leaders are prone to be removed or substituted. To ensure your job security in the future, you should be looking at

  - ☑ content and innovation-driven careers

  - ☑ expert roles or specialist career paths

  - ☑ Coaching and methodology-driven roles

- **You** may wish to consider that product management and product owner roles have more career progression potential, as they depend more on entrepreneurial competencies and the creation of innovation and product/market success than on the manager-to-staff ratio.

WE NEED MORE CLARITY ABOUT THE PROGRAMME; THEREFORE, WE DEMAND A [INSERT TITLE HERE] MANAGER.

We live in a world of interconnectivity. Technology makes use of different data sources to improve services, first at the local level but soon spreading change throughout the entire company. We are not able to draw a line, make a cut somewhere, start small and finish this piece before we move on.

I worked with one company on a project that contained four other projects that were somehow interconnected and interdependent. Into this setting a programme on top of it was introduced. Over time, this programme grew to contain seven projects. At this point, it had become so complex and unwieldy that timelines weren't able to contain all of the necessary information. As there was no way to get an overview of the project, people didn't know what was going on, and dependencies could no longer be solved.

> Fixing structural weaknesses with new roles or processes is pure patchwork.

The solution was to bring yet another expert on board. Although various experts had been brought in during the previous few months, this next expert would focus on something different and the programme would succeed. This person would be called the dependency manager, in honour of the cause of the problem.

After some time, it came to light that there was no longer anyone on the programme who was able to align releases into production. Hence another manager was appointed, and this person was named the release manager. One problem still remained. Due to the complexity, it had become untenable to oversee the whole process. Therefore, the end-to-end manager was brought in.

At this point, there were three new managers. They should have been asking themselves whether things were moving in the right direction. It occured to me like a typical Pattern. More manage ment people were brought into the programme. This leads to a higher amount of people on the programme. But it does not speed up its core, the very part of product development. Managers typically do not develop the product themselves, they govern or manage. This leads to more complexity, even though the intentions were right. After all, something still needed to be built, and none of these managers were able to do that. Sooner or later, having so many managers becomes a problem in itself.

In their Harvard Business Review article "Why Good Projects Fail Anyway", Nadim Matta and Ron Ashkenas write:

> [A]ttempting to achieve complex goals in fast-moving and unpredictable environments is humbling. Managers expect they will be able to identify, plan for, and influence all the variables and players in advance, but they can't.[88]

All of the misconceptions we have covered so far are clustered around the ideology that it is just about getting bigger, more complex, bringing in more people, securing more budget, finding excuses, and appointing scapegoats. Play your cards right, and all the numbers will be on your side. If things don't work out, blame someone else. Next time, you can approach it with all the things you will have learned from the mistakes. *Do we ever really learn from our mistakes? Or would we rather defend our errors in the interest of protecting our careers?*

---

[88] Matta, Nadim F. and Ron Ashkenas. "Why Good Projects Fail Anyway." *Harvard Business Review.* Sept. 2003 Issue. https://bit.ly/3kHe7c2

WHAT TO CONSIDER OR TRY NOW

- **Do** lessons-learned, retrospective or review sessions within any team and at any level—from the teams doing the work all the way up to management teams. Agree on actions and reserve time and budget to act on these. This will normally lead to improving practices, processes and roles. In modern Agile companies that have established structural and organisational Agility, it can even lead to changes to units, teams or moving team members.

- **Establish** and manage end-to-end value streams[89] instead of managing and co-ordinating projects or dependencies over several functional units. An end-to-end value stream manages the work from the moment the customer places the order request to the moment the customer receives the delivery. A focus on end-to-end flow means that the company actively manages this process throughout, with every role having accountability, functional alignment is secondary.

---

[89] "Value Streams." SAFe: Scaled Agile® Last updated 30 June 2020.
https://www.scaledagileframework.com/value-streams/

I HATE MY JOB, BUT I ENJOY THE PERKS.

While travelling to other places, learning new languages, and getting to know other cultures may provide a motivational boost, it is likely distracting you from the task at hand and it likely doesn't serve the company's best interests. Approaches such as near-shoring and off-shoring involve more countries in a project, so companies are able to send some colleagues there every so often. This provides employees with the opportunity to gain insight into other cultures while enjoying subsidised travel.

Speaking the native language of an overseas partner helps you to communicate more effectively and demonstrates your commitment to the partnership. There are always employees who are skilled at learning new languages and might enjoy going to the host country for a given time to learn it. While none of these practices is inherently evil, we have to be careful that we don't overdo it and lose focus on the task at hand.

At one company, I met a prime example of what I call the Jetsetter.

 Jessy Jetsetter - Frequent traveller. Travelling, moving with the projects. Never stops short for a new adventure.

He either travelled to a different location once per quarter or moved the project to a different country every other year. It seemed to me that he was placing her needs front and centre, instead of the company's success. When talking to people who travel for work, it is easy to tell whether they are engaging in essential travel or rather indulging themselves at the company's expense.

At the opposite end of the spectrum is the Homebody. The most extreme form of the Homebody insists on having a contract that is limited to their hometown even if typical company culture involves travel. Funnily enough, some of these people live more than an hour's journey from the company where they work.

Homer Homebody - king of his district. Everything Jessy Jetsetter is not. Work doesn't mean travelling for him, at all.

Even though their daily commute is already a huge pain, Homer Homebody is unwilling to add even an hour of extra travel to this. The employer might say: *What's another fifty minutes on top of your usual commute? This is just an occasional event.* Now or then, Homer will flat-out refuse. I have to wonder why the Homer signed the contract in the first place. Something like this was bound to come up sooner or later, and it is only for a limited amount of time.

Such obstacles are hard to overcome. Solving these problems requires time to be invested by the parties involved, and they do not add any value to the product itself. These little rebellions serve to divert energy from the project. In this sense, the Homebody is just as detrimental as the Jetsetter is to the common goal of creating value for the customer.

Another trademark of the Homebody is that they persist in speaking their native language, even if that isn't the official language of the company or of the project. Let's say that the company's official language is English. The Homebody switches to English only when the situation absolutely demands it. As the Homebody usually doesn't speak English well enough to communicate effectively in it, problems soon arise.

This is particularly striking in a corporate company that claims global status and has most likely appointed English as its primary conversational language years ago, yet its employees don't comply with this requirement. In many cases, this comes back to a human resources issue. Unless the appropriate organisational body enforces this requirement including supporting personnel in learning English, the company is failing to remove the practical roadblocks as well as undermining the importance of the directive. The time and money saved in the short term will incur a greater cost further down the line. A company will find itself at a massive disadvantage unless its employees can communicate effectively. Therefore, it's crucial to acquire language skills, but it's important to strike a balance.

WHAT TO CONSIDER OR TRY NOW

- **Working** abroad can be viewed through different lenses. Every advantage may have a flipside. Being thoroughly prepared and informed are key, just as is checking what is expected and whether it fits to your needs and targets:

    ☑ While it can be helpful to learn a language abroad, placing yourself in a situation where you cannot succeed without already having mastered the language is stressful and doesn't serve to advance your career.

    ☑ While you may earn more money abroad, keep in mind that the cost of living may be higher.

    ☑ While it may benefit you to work overseas, where you'll learn to adapt to a new culture, language, and various kinds of people and challenges, consider whether there will be the right mix of location, type of job, level, and team members available when it's time to return home.

RELEVANCE IS ALWAYS CORRELATED WITH SIZE.

It would seem simple enough, at first glance. The higher the stakes, the higher the revenue. It's worth taking huge risks—as long as things turn out well. Put something in motion and wait for it to snowball. If we are making great progress on a project, and the project is considered to be successful, the project grows and more requirements come in. To be able to handle them, we are required to add more resources to the project. We need more money to be able to pay additional people to work on the job.

It appears that just when we are doing a good job, more requirements are added to the project, which places a strain on us and our resources. If bigger is better, it would follow that the longer a project runs, the more job security there is for everyone involved. Therefore, the project scope is extended. If we're lucky, we'll also have sufficient budget and personnel added to the project. We believe that, with time, we can iron out the problems and overcome the hurdles. But has this approach ever really worked?

> Successful people know when to say *no*.

Instead of putting the money towards making the project ever bigger, wouldn't it be wiser to move at a steady pace?

Additional budget is allocated to the project, yet we continuously ask for more. Why? We want to add more people, so we can work at a faster pace and accomplish more within a shorter time. At the start of the project, as we hadn't factored everything into our calculations, we thought 20 percent dedication of our resources would be enough. The project itself has to be fed. We have to ensure that the project continues to grow, because we can only justify asking for more budget if there are more requirements to fulfil.

This snowballing will lead to the inevitable downfall of the project, because it will become untenable. Investing more money gives rise to higher expectations, and more people and requirements become involved, which increases the likelihood of producing inaccurate and failure-prone results. Despite hearing countless such stories, the reputation of a project manager still tends to hinge on the sheer size of the project and its budget.

WHAT TO CONSIDER OR TRY NOW

- **Be aware** of two proven facts:
  - ☑ The larger the project, the lower the success rate.[90]
  - ☑ The longer the timeframe of the project, the lower the success rate.[91]

---

[90] Bloch, Michael, Sven Blumberg, and Jürgen Laartz. "Delivering large-scale IT projects on time, on budget, and on value." 1 October 2012. *McKinsey Digital.* Accessed 27 July 2020. https://mck.co/3iKzUxL

[91] Stevenson, D.H. & Starkweather, J.A. "The impact of project duration on IT project success factors." ResearchGate. January 2011. https://bit.ly/2PWE3SY

09 | SAME BUT DIFFERENT

I HAVE ENCOUNTERED A DIFFERENT TYPE OF CHALLENGE OCCUR-ring most often within public agencies. A few factors distinguish public agencies from private companies, including greater potential for publicity, on one hand, and financial restrictions, on the other. In some cases, staff turnover occurs at an exceptionally high rate, while in other cases, the majority of personnel may remain with them for many years, merely decades. Both of these scenarios have their pros and cons.

Public agencies themselves tend to have customers from the government side, which makes budget discussions all the more complicated. And, as discussed in a previous chapter, they are often rather wasteful with their budgets (in terms of results, not daily rates - we will come to this later). As this is tax money, which belongs to you and me, I am keen to point that out, especially in front of my distinguished project colleagues at such companies. When you, as a concerned taxpayer, express disapproval of the way money is spent on the project, you are faced with silence and disbelief.

seems to me that many government officials are largely unaware that their responsibility extends beyond simply carrying out a job. They have a duty and an obligation to be resourceful and cautious with taxpayers' money. Everyone who works for government agencies, including those who are subcontracted to work on their projects, should be striving to make our society and our world a better place. Are we conscious of this fact?

THE OPERATING MODEL MUST BE SIMPLE, SO OUR CLIENT WILL UNDERSTAND AND APPROVE IT.

When a public agency requested my assistance with a project that hadn't worked out according to plan, it all appeared fairly straightforward at first. The problem seemed to stem from a mismanaged attempt to incorporate an Agile way of working right in the middle of a critical project. We didn't know that, in this country and within this agency, an Agile approach is considered to be just another project management framework. Employees implemented only the elements they considered to be helpful. In effect, this meant that they implemented only the elements that they understood, as people don't tend to consider something helpful unless they understand it.

> People will implement only what they understand.

As we've already discussed, with business implementation of Agile or any other change initiative, handpicking only the pieces with which you are familiar will not sustainably change the system; it will change certain factors without addressing the real root causes.

WHAT TO CONSIDER OR TRY NOW

■ **Some** thoughts on changing your horse mid-stream, so to speak:

☑ As Fred Brooks, the American computer architect, software engineer and computer scientist, writes in the Mythical Man-Month: "Adding people to an already late project delays it further."[92] This applies also when changing frameworks or methodologies.

☑ A common misconception is that Agile is a methodology. As compared to many widely known project-management methodologies, Agile is a mindset, described by a set of values and principles. When a methodology such as scrum implements these values and principles, it is called an Agile methodology.

☑ Most things we commonly call methodologies are fairly complex to understand and apply. Therefore, it is advisable to get a subject-matter expert on board to help you tailor it.

■ **When** it comes to deciding who does what and how to distribute work to various units, there are two very helpful models. These were designed by two competing strategic consultancy firms, BCG and McKinsey. Both models distinguish work by two factors relating to the type of work: repetitive/predictable versus variable/conceptional; and internal/operational versus customer facing. Depicting these factors as scales along an x and y axis there are between four and eight different working models.[93] Each of them belongs to a dedicated team (model) which can be either managed best by a lean or Agile team management model. Bear in mind: Building teams means deciding on the team management model and the type of work they do.

---

[92] Brooks, Fred. *Mythical Man Month: Essays on Software Engineering.* Addison-Wesley, 1975.

[93] Raedemaecker, Stefan, et al. "Lean Management or Agile? The Right Answer May B■ Both." *McKinsey & Co.* 14 July 2020. https://mck.co/2PXqNxf

WE ARE FUNDED BY OUR CUSTOMERS.
TURNING DOWN PROJECTS IS NOT AN OPTION.

Within the typical project-driven company, every demand from the client initiates a new project. For each new project, several roles have to be staffed, responsibilities need to be assigned, funding secured, and a single person must be appointed to be responsible for the project itself.

In the public sector, in particular, a specific situation arises, whereby the department responsible for creating the IT solution is not just another department that requires funding; it is a company founded expressly to serve the various businesses and therefore is prohibited from making a profit. Inexorably, receiving funding without having the opportunity to actually make money creates a dependency on the hand that feeds you. The client is asking for lower costs, optimised handling of issues, and quicker results, and the company is forced to meet these demands. This happens when one party simply funds projects while the other exists solely to deliver what's requested.

As well as serving your master (the client), you have to deal with the technology becoming obsolete (unless you make the necessary investments), employee demands (salary and career progression), company growth (expand the workforce or automate tasks). Turning down funding isn't an option, and as the projects pile up, people start to lose sight of the bigger picture. Everyone is focused on solving the problems at hand rather than on building the long-term success of the company.

It is easy to hide behind standards, standard solutions or generic methods.

When everyone is spread so thin, it is hard to find time to meet with other team members to go over details, flag up any issues, and test various solutions. This issue tends to be compounded by a lack of leadership. When everyone in the company is too overwhelmed by the scale of their projects or too busy juggling various projects to concentrate on the task at hand, everyone is a guest on all of their projects, so no one takes the initiative to push things forward and properly see things through.

WHAT TO CONSIDER OR TRY NOW

- **We** often begin projects without having a clear vision of what we are targeting. There are always some business objectives, but if they are phrased too abstract and intangible or if they too closely resemble the last project's objectives (e.g., increase speed, usability, etc.), they can be difficult for the members of the project teams to grasp. They need to see a meaningful vision of your ambitions for the project.

- **A North Star** vision is something you visualise so clearly in your mind that you can recreate that world. Expressing such a vision enables you to align your energy, emotions and actions in service of bringing this vision to life. The author and motivational speaker Simon Sinek established some ground rules for qualifying such a vision, which he calls a Just Cause. For him, a Just Cause must be:

  - ☑ **For something:** affirmative and optimistic

  - ☑ **Inclusive:** open for all to contribute

  - ☑ **Service oriented:** addresses universal need

  - ☑ **Resilient:** able to endure change

  - ☑ **Idealistic:** big, bold and ultimately unachievable

I HAVE FOLLOWED MY JOB DESCRIPTION TO THE LETTER.

When people aren't fully engaged, they may simply go through the motions without applying analytical or critical thought as to why these measures are being applied.

In a case study presented earlier, the rescue strategy was to bring in a new project management technique, commence working towards automation, implement new status reporting and introduce new roles and responsibilities. On paper, this plan seems flawless, yet we failed to meet the objective, and that's what matters.

> Everyone on the project should take ownership and accountability for their outcomes.

You can do everything right according to a methodology, and still get it wrong. Going through the motions won't create the desired results when there are underlying issues preventing people from understanding what they are doing. All too often, the rationale behind such steps is that it is being done to serve the bosses: *Yes, we implemented this new standard, therefore everything must be right.* To paraphrase one employee: *We planned the suggested number of work packages, and they have been structured according to protocol. I believe we are right on track.*

According to the methodology framework and the standards, they were doing everything right. However, in all this time, they had failed to carry out these three things:

- No one talked about the product to be built; they discussed only the measures and the planning.

- There was no direct communication between the teams building the product; all contact was conducted via intermediaries.

- No one ever thought to check which capabilities the newly created product already had.

This was a textbook case of simply following standards or the orders to do so. They had mindlessly followed the processes without applying any analytical thought processes. They had not challenged assumptions, nor had they tried to understand or solve the underlying problems. Only looking forward, never looking back, and not speaking with the people involved is a recipe for disaster.

In the end within a single project, they managed to accumulate more issues than I would have ever imagined possible. It just goes to show that programme and project governance continue to be of utmost importance. How much governance would it take to ensure constant progress? During this project, the lack of discernible progress necessitated increasing levels of governance and so following further bureaucratic process steps.

Eventually, the company was forced to apply the brakes. It split the projects into independent sections and immediately terminated half of them. This was perhaps one of the best decisions made in the course of the project lifetime but required months of deliberation.

WHAT TO CONSIDER OR TRY NOW

- **It's easy** to get caught up in trying to master our processes, tools and documentation. We sometimes project our anxiety about our tasks onto these instruments, which exist to help us to achieve our desired outcomes. They are simply the means to an end. That's why the Agile Manifesto recommends taking a more conscious and streamlined approach to implementing methods, tools, and documentation. Every time you plan to introduce one of these elements into your specific setting, ask yourself the following questions:

  ☑ How does it help me to achieve my targeted objectives (e.g., standard of quality, amount of scope, adhering to deadlines)?

☑ Is it redundant? Do I already have something that fulfils this need?

☑ Can I achieve the same result by introducing or using something which requires less effort?

■ **When** running product or service development projects, apply these principles so as to remain holistic, effective and efficient:

☑ Centre the customer: Involve your customer and provide value to your customer

☑ Test and evaluate product or service and its user acceptance early and often

☑ Measure what matters and leave out the rest: Choose metrics that focus on customer value

☑ Build in quality rather than testing it in

☑ Data is your friend—base your decisions on facts or fact-based metrics.

READ THE FINE PRINT! IT'S NEVER OUR FAULT.

The need for a contract is quite a peculiar thing, if you really think about it. In this day and age, we cannot seal the deal with a handshake, because we do not know or trust our collaborators. All too often, the rifts between departments or organisations run so deep that signing a contract is more than a formality.

At one time, Carey was working for a company we'll call ITCo, who has a client company we'll call BusCo. The two companies are legally bound to each other. In fact, ITCo was founded by BusCo and as a supplier is the de facto IT department. In this roles ITCo delivers solutions for all sorts of demands. These include office solutions, such as text processing or e-mail; off-the-shelf software, such as CRM or BI solutions; and custom-developed specific solutions.

BusCo requested new digitisation products and Carey took over responsibility for this deal. She was kind enough to provide us with the background story. Until five years ago, all of BusCo's business departments either had their own IT departments or would outsource this work. As a result, it sometimes happened that one external supplier would find themselves dealing separately with different departments within the organisation. This meant that they would pitch their ideas independently to these departments and would offer them different prices. And, as they were using a range of different vendors, some incompatibility issues arose between departments. Some departments were developing internal solutions on their own while other departments were buying off-the-shelf solutions.

Not only did this compound the incompatibility issues, it confused matters further when it came to their workforce strategy. Some departments were paying for IT personnel, whereas others were saving costs on the personnel front while racking up considerable expense on the outsourcing part. As no synergy effects could be used, IT personnel were shared across departments, which necessitated even more complicated processes. To address these problems, BusCo established a new company, ITCo, whose sole purpose is to define, buy and build IT solutions for the business departments.

Now, they're hoping to build a truly marvellous product that provides the solutions to all kinds of issues faced by consumers. BusCo wishes to make it leaner, slicker, and easier to use; ITCo promises to bring it right to the cutting edge. However, both companies have had disastrous experiences in the past. Projects have failed. Deals have fallen through at the last minute. As a result, each has deep-rooted negative feelings and they mistrust one another. BusCo and ITCo don't want to work with each other, but they have no choice. It's a *can't live with them, can't live without them* situation.

They work together, but each party is coming from a place of suspicion and paranoia that prevents open communication. BusCo micromanages and second-guesses ITCo, while ITCo blocks transparency and withholds information from BusCo. Instead of finding common ground, both sides are operating in a defensive manner. The project concludes in an all-too-familiar battle about requirements.

BusCo says: *The brief was crystal-clear, yet you have not delivered on time, so you should deliver the project at no extra cost.*

ITCo responds: *We would have delivered on time if you had not changed the project's scope so many times. You kept adding new requests that required us to make a lot of supporting changes behind the scenes. You fail to recognise the extra work we've carried out, even though you will benefit greatly from it.*

A company who finds itself in this position will usually appoint a representative or a project manager to take care of the dirty work. Here's where Carey steps in. She is perfectly cut out to play this role. She starts out by making excuses, finding loopholes, and apportioning blame. Then, she brokers a new agreement, builds in buffers, and pushes through her company's demands.

If Carey isn't available or if she requires back-up, a team of various managers will step in to apply pressure to the other party. Carey will handle the negotiations and takes the heat if something goes wrong. Such processes can make life easier for the company in question, the downside being that they are time-consuming and require documentation and negotiation material.

To quote W. Edwards Deming, "A system must be managed. […] Left to themselves […] components [of the system] become selfish, competitive. We cannot afford the destructive effect of competition."[94]

When we create structures that function independently as teams or departments, with separate missions and KPIs, these structures will do everything within their power to optimise themselves. This works well except in cases where the objective requires these structures to collaborate. If these structures independently create their KPIs, they can end up contradicting each other. You will need to properly align the overall objectives and appoint an authority to oversee handling the trade-offs, as well as any conflicts that may arise.

This is where the objectives and key results (OKR) framework and methodology (which we discussed in **Chapter 6: Culture Eats Strategy for Breakfast**) comes in useful. As well as providing support in highlighting contradictions and other areas where collaboration and co-ordination are required, it can help you to manage these for the greater good of the project and the organisation as a whole.

[94] Deming, W. Edwards. *The New Economics for Industry, Government, Education.* MIT Press, 2000.

WHAT TO CONSIDER OR TRY NOW

- **The** power of value stream management is that it places governance and target alignment processes directly in the hands of those who manage the value stream from end to end—from customer request to customer delivery. Naturally, corresponding business and IT departments belonging to one common value stream are intertwined, even in team structures, and coordinated at the highest levels by one leadership team.[95]

- **Beyond** solutions relying on fixing the structures or processes, we always have to look at the human side. In The Trusted Advisor, David Maister, Charles Green and Robert Galford present a trust equation, in which the variables of credibility, reliability, intimacy and self-orientation interact to produce a trust quotient.[96] We should strive to optimise the first three elements, of which intimacy is most often neglected; and to minimise self-orientation, which includes selfish behaviour that is not centred on the client's welfare in the long term.

- **Another** beautiful model comes from Patrick Lencioni's book *The Five Dysfunctions of a Team: A Leadership Fable.* Similar to Maslow's hierarchy of needs, the Lencioni Trust Pyramid visualises the five elements of trust in order of essentiality and how each layer forms the basis for the next one.[97]

---

[95] "Value Stream Coordination." SAFe: Scaled Agile® Last updated 25 June 2020. https://www.scaledagileframework.com/value-stream-coordination/

[96] Maister, David, Green Charles H. & Robert M. Galford. *The Trusted Advisor.* Free Press, 2000.

[97] Lencioni, Patrick. *The Five Dysfunctions of a Team: A Leadership Fable.* Jossey-Bass, 2002.

WE CAN'T AFFORD TO BRING IN SENIOR PERSONNEL. LET'S BRING IN SOME JUNIOR PERSONNEL INSTEAD.

For many years, this strategy has been applied across various professions. When administered in moderation, it is beneficial for all parties concerned. The benefits of involving people of varying levels of seniority and experience on a project include the following:

- The consulting company profits from having a range of expertise and perspectives in its teams.

- The more senior members of the team benefit from having a fresh outlook and additional assistance.

- The client receives more varied levels of consulting, yielding greater engagement and empathy, and more down-to-earth conversations.

- Junior personnel gain valuable experience at an early stage in their careers.

That being said, I don't endorse the practice of flooding teams with junior employees for the purpose of cutting costs. Their lack of experience will invariably start to show and there will be a shortage of senior staff to support them. This will eventually lead to lower quality of the product. In the long run, no one will benefit.

Blending various levels of experience in a team is beneficial for all parties.

The external company is training its personnel at the client's expense and on the client's time. After the project is completed, the client company will have trained a fleet of personnel that is not going to remain with it. The client will be forced to repeat the cycle with different staff and /or consulting company. Cutting corners is always a false economy, as it will end up costing you dearly, in terms of reputation, relationships, people development, and quality.

WHAT TO CONSIDER OR TRY NOW

- **To gauge** levels of experience, competency and skill, you can use the Dreyfus Model.[98] It is a classification assessment defining five levels of skills acquisition as follows: *novice; advanced beginner; competent; proficient;* and *expert.* It then identifies the style of recollection, recognition, decision and awareness associated with each of these levels.

  - ☑ For our purposes, we can define a novice as someone who may have only heard of a concept, and

  - ☑ a beginner as someone who is trained in this concept and may have observed it applied in at least one real project situation without being an integral part of it.

  - ☑ A competent person has actively worked in such an environment while occupying a learning role and thus still being somewhat dependent.

  - ☑ A proficient person can work independently with a concept and advises others in certain areas.

  - ☑ An expert has worked with the concept in several situations and has introduced it to others and provided advice based upon their experience and knowledge.

- **The** calculation of a manager-to-staff ratio for setting up teams seems to be an art rather than a function. There are some known and measurable factors (e.g., type of work performed, supervisor versus employee ability, rank/span of control, variation, costs) to be considered when calculating the optimal ratio for any given situation, usually somewhere between a 1:4 to 1:20. [99]

---

[98] "Dreyfus Model of Skill Acquisition." Wikipedia. Last modified 18 June 2020. https://bit.ly/2G0vdSg

[99] Weiss, Dyanne. "Ideal Ratio of Managers to Staff." Azcentral. Updated 5 April 2018. https://bit.ly/342Ih4N

PART B:
**DIFFERENT
PERSPECTIVES**

ALTHOUGH INCORPORATING CHANGE IN organisations bears some similarities across the board, it varies somewhat from one industry to the next, so I feel it is valuable to hear about other experiences. I invited experts from various industries to contribute guest chapters sharing their views on corporate change and how they address it in their respective fields. This section is introduced by Christoph Lechner, Sales Director at Scoot & Ride GmbH (http://www.scootandride. com), who offers valuable insight from another industry perspective.

10 | **IT ALWAYS STARTS
AT THE BEGINNING**

By Christoph Lechner

A S I READ THIS BOOK, I FOUND MYSELF SHAKING MY HEAD IN disbelief more often than I would have liked. I really wonder how it can be that so many things are going wrong in organisations and projects. In my point of view—sorry, Henrik—there really ought to be no need to write such a book.

My career is fundamentally disparate from Henrik´s, and this is certainly one of the reasons why he has invited me to contribute my views on this subject. I have spent almost my entire professional life in small companies, typically comprising between one and thirty-five employees. Today, I am extremely lucky to be one of the co-owners of a growth company (which was initially a start-up), distributing children's scooters in fifty-six countries across all five continents. Our scooter brand is currently the fourth largest globally; in some countries we are the leading brand. Our headquarters is located in Upper Austria, and at present we have nine employees. Although that may sound small to you, we serve, and work and negotiate with, a wide range of shareholders: our employees; eight investors; a number of banks; three production sites in China and Vietnam; fifty-one distributors; five sales agents; around twenty key accounts; and, in total, around fifteen thousand shops—both of the online and brick-and-mortar variety—worldwide.

ACT AS THOUGH IT IS YOUR OWN COMPANY.

Being a co-owner of this company allows me (most often, but not always) to do things the way I want to do them. In a nutshell, my style of work is straightforward and challenges the status quo. I sincerely believe that employees should look at the company for whom they work as if it is their very own.

> ❝❝
> Don't let the prevailing culture destroy your company.

These are the three key principles I seek to imprint upon all of our applicants during the job interview, and again on their very first working day (and at a later date, if necessary):

1 | **We cannot afford to tell you what to do and I will not do so.** We are looking for independently thinking employees who support our long-term goals and want to achieve something on their own initiative. I am here to guide you in this direction.

2 | **If you see something that is going bad, make it better.** Even more so, if this thing was introduced by one of the founders (including me). Oh, and don't forget to tell me about it—I also want to learn.

3 | **If you make a mistake, correct it.** Inform me if I need to know about it; if not, then don't.

As what I am about to say may sound harsh, please rest assured that I intend it in the kindest and most encouraging way. And while it may sound a bit too straightforward, it cuts to the core of the dissociative attitudes I have observed in many companies, particularly the large ones.

- Employees act like the company is an entity that's separate from their employment.

- Employees act like they can´t achieve anything on their own.

- Employees act like the company is run by somebody other than them.

It's almost as if there is a weird separation, with the employees and their tasks on one side and the company on the other.

Although I don't have much experience as an employee in large companies, a number of our customers are large companies. On several occasions, I have seen employees doing the following:

- Avoiding taking over responsibility due to fear of the consequences of making a bad decision

- Delaying decisions past the point where everybody forgot about the decision to be made in first place

- Avoiding taking on a project because this would mean having to fight for it internally

- Blaming others for their failures, instead of being accountable for their own actions

From where do these attitudes stem? What is the real reason employees feel that they are a separate entity from the company for whom they work? Why don't they realise they are part of a group that is working to achieve a shared goal?

We have a saying in Austria that goes: *Der Fisch stinkt immer vom Kopf.* "The fish always starts to smell from the head." What this really means is that the fish always starts to smell from the beginning.

Here, at the beginning, the roots of all problems are to be found. Here, at the very beginning, the company culture, the norms and values, the core principles are unwittingly introduced. Here is the place where all future behaviour and prevailing attitudes are shaped. Here is the formation of an enterprise.

That's why, if you want to blame somebody for all that is going wrong, you should blame the founders. Blame the people, like me, who shaped the company, because we are the ones who hired the first employees, who typically are highly like-minded, and who will hire the next employees, and so on.

"Every system is perfectly designed to get the results it gets."

–W. Edwards Deming

In an ideal world, the beginning is the place and time to start enacting change. This is the reason why I try to drum the abovementioned three key principles into the mind of every new employee like a church prayer. I want to create a regulatory, a counterpart, so that many people, instead of a select few, create the culture together. This keeps the culture alive, transformable, and active. Hopefully this helps us avoid forming a company culture that is written in stone and will never change again. I think all companies should try to implement such a regulatory as well, right from the beginning. (I am fully aware that this is easier said than done. Circle back to me in a few years, and I can tell you how it's working out.)

Let's say you are facing a situation where you have to implement something new in a company. Your task is to make a change, to introduce something new to a firmly established culture, which has grown organically and is playing by its own rules. These rules were set in place years ago, and everyone in the company has become accustomed to them. Yes, everyone kind of likes them. The best-case scenario is that you are facing fear and resistance because, let's face it, who of us really likes externally imposed change? The worst-case scenario is that nobody pays any attention to you.

You can´t go back in time to change the company culture to a more flexible one. So you try it the hard way, by breaking up these rules and this culture. You will soon find that this is next to impossible, as they are too deeply ingrained within the DNA of the company. Is there a better, simpler way?

INTRAPRENEURSHIP AND CORPORATE ENTREPRENEURSHIP

Intrapreneurship describes a transformation in employee behaviour that moves towards more responsibility, independent action, and active design, towards entrepreneurial behaviour.

Corporate entrepreneurship means that the dynamic of entrepreneurship that exists when the company is created is successfully anchored in the long-term culture of the company. In my opinion, this is the ideal approach, though I am not sure if it is achievable.

Whether we are talking about intrapreneurship or corporate entrepreneurship, entrepreneurial behaviour should ultimately be the goal. There are many successful examples of both of these types of entrepreneurial behaviour, and in the end the distinction between them is not that important. Any kind of initiative that increases employee ownership over tasks and responsibilities, and breaks up entrenched structures and processes, obsolete communication channels, and so on, should be encouraged and demanded, even though this will likely incur some amount of inconvenience and subject you to ridicule, and possibly make you unpopular.

To give you an example of what I mean by entrepreneurial behaviour, I heard a very interesting anecdote the other day about a woman who has recently started fresh at a new company. She works in the legal department, advising from the legal perspective on the possibility to enter new markets. She noticed that the employment contract offered by the company contains a number of flaws that should be corrected. This does not fall under her job description, nor is it particularly interesting for her. Nevertheless, she has taken it upon herself to suggest changes to the contract. At the time of writing, it's too early to tell whether or not her project was successful, but I can tell you that it is precisely this type of involvement that makes a difference.

IT HURTS!

In conclusion, I'd like to tell you about my biggest learning experience. Only once in my life did I ever sincerely want to work for a big company. The position entailed a very interesting sounding area of responsibility, a very good compensation package, and an international orientation. During the job interview, I was surprised to hear the vice president of human resources telling me that she did not believe that this company would be the right place for me. Nevertheless, I got the job and—spoiler alert—I lasted there for twenty-six days.

The problem was not my co-workers, my superiors, nor the payment. The problem was the company culture. Every little detail had to be coordinated with the CEO. Every idea, every change, every deviation from the norm had to be coordinated with him. Logically, 99.9 percent of all ideas, changes, deviations never reached the CEO. It was (and may still be) an old culture. There was no room for initiative or self-fulfilment.

As I said, I quit twenty-six days after my first day of work. After the first week, I already knew I would do so. At my termination interview, the vice president of human resources told me she was not at all surprised—quite the contrary. She had predicted it, after all. In confidence, she told me that she had been hoping that, by bringing in a new kind of spirit, she could change the prevailing company culture for the better.

To all the CEOs, to all the company founders, to all the top management folks out there: You don't want (and nor can you afford) to have a company that consists only of people who say yes to everything you say. What you want and need are people with their own ideas who want to achieve something on their own initiative. You have to step back and give them the space to do so. Even if it hurts.

THE HUMAN
ELEMENT

By Regina Gruber

W HAT EXACTLY IS CHANGE? AND WHAT EXACTLY DOES change within a company entail? We know that change plays out uniquely within each company, but what is the defining factor that influences these respective differences? Is it the company's size, its personnel or the specific projects it undertakes?

In recent years, I have been recurrently confronted with this question, particularly when I myself have been involved in projects or when I have noted personnel or departmental changes occurring as a result of projects. That's what my job as a human resources manager is all about.

At the end of the day, the human resource is not simply pure resource. Above all, it is a sum of feelings, character traits, characteristics, talents, values, and experiences. Every project requires on the people involved; every company is filled with people

Therefore, every kind of change is also shaped by these people. The success of any project and its associated changes depends on these very feelings, values, and experiences.

Closely connected to this is the corporate culture, which describes the values, norms and attitudes that effectively shape the decisions, actions and behaviour of the members of a company. It also encompasses how a company is structured, which role each person plays, which functions are performed within specific departments, and how the business levels interact. A company that is committed to growth and development also recognises that change is important and engenders a culture in which change processes can succeed. The only certainty is that change is inevitable. And that is why change is part of the corporate culture.

Clearly, the values and rules in effect within companies (and their projects) help to shape the corporate (and project) culture. Ultimately, these values—which may include fairness, trust, critical faculties, loyalty, and performance orientation—strongly influence the performance of a company and its projects. Equally, this determines how the people in the company interact and communicate with each other.

In this book, Henrik Gruber extensively describes some of the less exemplary human behaviour he has observed within corporations, including the exercise of power and the political games. A German term immediately comes to mind: Es menschelt. This expression means that wherever there is a chaotic and miserable mass of human beings, all their feelings, weaknesses and faults will inevitably surface. I would like to draw your attention to an element that Henrik omits to mention. In every corporation, one central department centres the soft factor called a human being. This is the human resources (HR) department.

THE ROLE OF HR MANAGEMENT IN A CHANGE PROCESS

Over the last two decades, the function of the human resources department has altered considerably. This is due to the changing dynamics and ever-increasing pace of society, caused by transparency, globality, and the Internet, among other factors. While the mundane tasks (such as administration, recruiting, personnel development, and the like) are nowadays more often regarded as the daily business of a human resource manager, I believe you can recognise a good HR department by the extent to which it is involved in corporate decisions. We are seeing a trend whereby the role of the HR manager is moving away from that of an executive and administrator to that of a (pro)active (co-)creator and strategist.

With his HR model in 1997, the American business professor author, speaker and management coach Dave Ulrich already anticipated these changes in personnel work. He defined four central roles as follows[100]:

1. **Administrative Expert:** bears responsibility for efficient implementation of HR processes; drives infrastructure design
2. **Employee Champion:** fosters higher performance; cultivates higher commitment
3. **Strategic Partner:** co-ordinates HR activities; anticipate future developments
4. **Change Agent:** accompanies change/transformation; empowers individual employees

One of the main roles of the HR manager during a change project is similar to the role of the Change Agent. A Change Agent represents the mediators and facilitators in change processes. Th

---

[100] Ulrich, Dave. *Human Resource Champions the next Agenda for Adding Value and Delivering Results. Boston*, MA: Harvard Business School Press, 1997.

Change Agent is the link between management and personnel. Via the structured work of the Change Agent, employees are proactively involved and thus made fit for change. A Change Agent in HR, for example, recognises trends and developments, adapts competence requirements for employees, and qualifies them according to the change.

However, one must not forget that employees in the HR department are permanently engaged within a field of tension. Therefore, they often experience role conflicts. Regardless of how strongly they are involved with a change process, and even if they are proactively driving it, they must never forget the following factors:

- They must maintain their neutrality. Interfering in conflicts and power games or the allocation of competencies, must only be based on facts.

- Although they work with and for people, they should remain objective. Emotions have no place in the supporting role.

- It is especially important to be proactive by disclosing one's own motivation, development and vision. This also makes you a co-creator as an employee of the HR department.

- The main goal—the successful completion of a project or change—must not be neglected. All other interests are therefore considered secondary, but not unimportant. It's essential to maintain that balance.

Another important role of the HR department is that of the strategist. The value of an HR department within a corporation stands and falls with the recognition of the value of HR work. This refers to the involvement of the personnel management in the development of the strategy. The HR department is equally responsible for the success of the company at all levels and towards all stakeholders.

In summary, the role of a good and strong HR department is very similar to that of a consultant, coach, mediator, moderator, motivator or driver for change.

SUCCESSFUL SUPPORT BY THE HR DEPARTMENT

This book describes in detail many of the common pitfalls and mistakes encountered in change initiatives. As I read it, I frequently said to myself: "That's right! That's what happened to me, too." Or: "Oh yes, that's what we forget every time we plan a project." This is exactly what I believe this book really is—a summary of the hurdles and challenges, which ideally should be recorded on the project map in advance of every project or change initiative. In order to clearly define or, at least, to mitigate the stumbling blocks before embarking upon a project.

Unfortunately, this happens far too rarely. Why is this the case? Probably because there is not enough time or because a project is not considered to be important enough to warrant it. Furthermore, people are involved throughout the process. When people take action and stir things up, something happens around them and others can sense this as well. There are always side effects and consequences involved.

We can discuss this in terms of a real-life example. Just under two years ago, one particular company restructured its entire European sales department with the ambitions of driving the successful development of the company and achieving associated growth in sales. The objectives were clear: to further increase efficiency, transparency, customer orientation, and, consequently, sales.

In this case, the role of the HR department was primarily that of the Change Agent mentioned above. When the managers of the sales department first considered the idea of restructuring, the HR department was immediately informed and thus invited to collaborate in the positive developments. Together with the managers, the HR department theoretically analysed the new structure, and reviewed and partly redefined all existing titles and roles. This also resulted in career advancements for certain individuals. The preparation for this change entailed a clearly structured and comprehensive communication plan. This included one-on-one interviews with employees, and discussions with entire departments during the restructuring process. The plan also clearly outlined what was to be communicated, at which time, by whom, and using which words. Furthermore, considerations were already done for the phase after the restructuring and the corresponding communication and support afterwards.

When everyone was in agreement, the implementation started. They informed all the people affected by the initiative, executed the communication plan, sent out new organisational charts, and applied the job promotions and salary adjustments. Above all, the role of the HR department as Change Agent was to support communication, not least because it is an intermediary between employees, managers, and other stakeholders. It coordinates and links everyone in the company through this very interface.

The HR employees attended many ongoing meetings of the restructuring, participated in meetings with departments and employees, and co-ordinated the exchange between employees. While they faced many questions and much critical feedback from some of the parties involved, listening and providing transparency made a big difference. Together they managed to present the restructuring initiative as something consistently positive and to gain strong support for the change itself.

Directly after the implementation, individual HR employees were assigned to regularly communicate with managers and employees. Through targeted questions and coaching sessions, they captured and documented the thoughts, experiences and concerns of the managers and employees. In addition, electronically anonymised surveys were conducted periodically, which also reflected the mood in the departments. This enabled them to take further targeted measures, such as joint events, redefinition of rules and regulations, and documentation and publication of role descriptions.

THE PREDICTABILITY OF CHANGE

As we've seen in the example provided above, change in a company is not always predictable or calculable. Frequently, unforeseen circumstances arise. Things happen from one day to the next, for example, through the exchange of managers, the reprioritisation of projects, or the change of cultures and values within the company. Companies commonly underestimate the far-reaching impact of projects or plans. These are not merely the implementation of a necessity, but also influence a large number of people and processes.

The aforementioned change in the sales structure was voluntary and planned. Nevertheless, a further change took place within this very structure, just under a year later. The economic crisis resulting from the effects of COVID-19 led to a more or less forced change. And when a change initiative is undertaken at such short notice and without much forward planning, it soon becomes evident that there is a lack of structure. People suddenly forget how a change project should be carried out. Why? Because an unpleasant situation that arises suddenly is often not viewed as a project at all, but as an obstacle or a short-term challenge, its overall scope is vastly underestimated. Everything that would clearly lead to a successful project conclusion and change initiative goes out the window. It menschelt. And that is, unfortunately, quite a normal state of affairs.

When orders suddenly started to decline, thus threatening sales growth, the management team decided to reverse much of the original restructuring. The goal was to save costs and therefore resources in order to still achieve the company's goals and performance indicators. From one day to the next, employees talked about rumoured blacklists for layoffs, and the works council asked the HR department for its opinion. Once again, the only way to react was to communicate. By the time the management team and the HR department had come to an agreement on the who, how and what of communication, so much tension had already built up within the company that important professionals took flight and the customers and partners of the company were faced with fear. Far too late, the realisation came to light that even a crisis should be considered a project, even though the reality clearly shows that a crisis involves many unpredictable factors that cannot be assessed and therefore cannot be planned in detail. Based on my experience, I can say that even a crisis labelled with a project name can be mastered successfully. The keys are neutrality, transparency and communication—the factors of the HR department set out above.

IN A CHANGE INITIATIVE, WHAT DEFINES SUCCESS?

In Part A of this book, Henrik Gruber describes in detail what defines a project as successful. In summary, based on his explanations, one could say the following:

A project is successful when:
- The content-wise objective has been achieved;
- the costs have remained within the budget; and
- the schedule has not been excessively strained.

At the same time, after reading this book, I once again identified one conclusion for me: change management happens every day and everywhere. Where people work or come together, something happens all the time. This means that change occurs everywhere—through communication, exchange, development and experience.

The involvement of a human resources department is primarily beneficial to the achievement of objectives in terms of content. In other words, through the proactive involvement of employees, clear communication and an understanding of humans as a resource, a hard project is acknowledged even with its soft aspects and leads to success. Conversely, this means that a change process is always designed by people. Henrik has already described this in detail. However, it is important to understand and recognise this from the very beginning. In a project, it *menschelt,* and the chances of success of a project increase if this human factor is taken into account. It must be clear from the very beginning that it is crucial to proactively involve the employees, and not only those who supervise or commission the change project, but also those who might be connected with it or feel its effects.

To quote Henrik once again, this is also about committed managers like Madeleine. Such an executive seeks advice and support in good time from the HR department and engages them as a sparring partner. Jointly, they can develop a clear project and communication plan and quickly involve all those affected, to gain as many early followers as possible. Resistance can be counteracted.

In the end, it is about the company in which a project and change initiative are implemented. Together we create new values, strengthen existing values, develop knowledge, drive innovation, wake up latent resources, and solve conflicts productively. And if you can do this successfully as a manager or project leader, it is not least because you had the Change Agents from the HR department with you, who strengthened your back.

HO O   O NH_2

HO O

12 | **AN EDGE ON THE COMPETITION**

By Patrick Malicek

WE LIVE IN A SERVICE SOCIETY AND MOST OF US OWN MORE than we need: one or two mobile phones and tablets, at least one laptop, and continuous internet connectivity. It is common to have two university diplomas; we have never known more than we do today. We high-flyers consume service offerings—ranging from food delivery and rental cars to online workshops—many times each day. *Why, then, do we still regularly fail as professional service providers?*

ALL SERVICE OFFERINGS ARE EQUAL

As service providers who want to stand out in today's market without offering the lowest price, the best way we can differentiate ourselves from the competition is by offering high-quality products. In this respect, the increasing homogenisation of the range of services is problematic. Because it is becoming increasingly difficult to differentiate, differentiation in the practical sense—from the customers' perspective—is achieved primarily through offering additional services[101].

Therefore, the key question is: How do I act if I, as a premium provider, have to charge premium market prices, and the customer assesses the quality of my service as being only of average quality?

In my experience, both the management and the employees of the service provider usually are mindful of the tension between price and quality of the service During the implementation of IT projects

Instead of doing as much as you can, do the things that count.

with external service providers, I have often observed that young professionals fresh out of university are invested mainly in building up their own technical and professional competence. But even experienced software architects of the Dillon type will often work hard to constantly expand already impressive repertoires with new, innovative architectural approaches, in order to use them with their customers, in keeping with the motto "a lot helps a lot". The management of these motivated employees backs this up firm-wide with certification initiatives and continuing education programmes, more than 95 percent of which are in the following areas of competence:

- technical
- professional
- methodological
- conceptual

This is short-sighted for two reasons. First, it precipitates disproportionate investment in the professional and technical

---

[101] Qualitätsmanagement für Dienstleistungen (Manfred Bruhn, Springer-Verlag GmbH Deutschland, 2019)

competences of one's own employees, in the belief that this is necessary to stand out to the customer in terms of service quality; and second, this is comparatively easy for competitors to imitate.

Because it has long since ceased to be enough to provide customers with good solutions according to agreement. Rather, the customer must be satisfied comprehensively, i.e. also subjectively verifiably. This is easier said than done, because while hard factors such as functionality or price can be verified comparatively reliably, guaranteeing soft factors such as cooperation in partnership and smooth communication is much more difficult[102].

Generally speaking, service employees—regardless of whether they are newcomers to the profession or experienced specialists—are primarily designated goals regarding their own service quality, while management employees are given economic success goals.

However, in the literature on the success chain of quality management[103], we see that there are four successive links, each of them building on the last and paving the way for the next as follows:

1. High quality of service
2. Customer satisfaction
3. Customer loyalty
4. Economic success

Who takes care of the two links in the middle, and how?

An even bigger issue, which is compounded by the fact that it is largely ignored, is that our customers do not only expect services to function with **professional, technical, methodological** and concep-

[102] Kundenzufriedenheit im IT-Outsourcing (Ferri Abolhassan, Springer Fachmedien Wiesbaden, 2014)

[103] Qualitätsmanagement für Dienstleistungen (Manfred Bruhn, Springer-Verlag GmbH Deutschland, 2019)

tual competences; they also have expectations of the experience of the service itself, with regards to **social** and **psychological** competences.

Of these competences, we tend to undervalue the latter two and do not do enough to promote them. Nor do we pay enough attention to the interpersonal relationships between our employees and our customers. We are failing to understand that this is what differentiates us from our competitors. It is not only about having knowledge—it's about our people and how they convey this knowledge to our customers.

THE CUSTOMER RELATIONSHIP IS A MARATHON, NOT A SPRINT

I work with my staff every day to address the core question posed at the beginning of this chapter. I encourage my consultants to speak directly with the customer. My goal is to reduce the tendency to approach customer situations with arrogance. External professionals and consultants often think they know exactly what a customer's problem is; however, while this may very well be true and they might have the right solution at hand, the customer may not be aware of the problem and may not perceive it as a pain point. This gives rise to the classic situation: we present solutions to questions that the customer is not yet asking. It may seem simple enough—all we have to do is engage them in a personal dialogue. Once we know what the pain points are, only then can we ascertain which competitive advantages need to be fulfilled from the customer's point of view. As a rule of thumb, any such advantage must be a significant core service that is particularly valued by the customer, and it must be designed with permanence, so that it cannot be imitated in the short term. In a direct conversation, one can form an overview of the customer's understanding of quality as follows

- Factual quality dimension (punctuality, reliability, accuracy)

- Personal quality dimension (openness, honesty, friendliness)

- Interpersonal quality dimension (flexibility, empathy, fairness)

The quality and viability of the relationship is assessed by the customer in a past-oriented way, in terms of familiarity (based on the time spent working together and the number of joint projects), as well as in a future-oriented way, in terms of trust (based on past experience that verifies a reliable standard and pattern of future behaviour). Therefore, when our experienced IT architect provides services for our customer, we would hope that he delivers value in as many dimensions as possible.

I don't know of any service provider who assigns its professionals or managers the goal of gaining a better understanding of their customers and provides them with the resources to help them achieve this. And yet, this is what we should do. Let's be honest—if we have a superficial interest in our customers and nurture these relationships only when we want to sell them a new service, why should they value us as trusted advisors?

MOMENTS OF TRUTH: A COMPETITIVE EDGE

When we engage in an honest conversation with a customer, we can expect to receive positive and negative feedback. I have often been in situations where the customer did not agree with the service provision because the clarification of an incident was insufficient during the project. Intuitively, I would immediately approach the customer to solve the problem that had arisen and strive to bring about a de-escalation in a timely manner through appropriate conflict management. Leaving things to fester always bears the risk of a lasting negative impact on the customer relationship. In certain scenarios, I have witnessed service providers citing serious errors from the customer's side, attempting to hush things up or condescending to the expert knowledge of the customers about their processes. Such cases invariably result in damaging the image of the company as a whole, and of the employees involved, in particular.

These moments of truth often determine whether a business relationship will live or die. Such a moment serves not only as an important indicator of the wellbeing of the customer relationship, it also offers an opportunity to positively differentiate oneself from the competition. A customer who communicates his concerns to the service provider is interested in further cooperation[104]. Concrete measures and programmes should be derived from all results and findings in order to sustainably increase customer satisfaction. The customer must feel the results. Only when the initiated measure is perceived positively by the customer is it considered to have been successfully implemented. In this context, employees constitute the most important link in the service chain. If customers are dissatisfied with a product, a service or an idea, this must be taken seriously even when those in the upper echelons confidently assure us that there is no reason for dissatisfaction and that the customer is only ungrateful or incompetent[105]. This negative casting presents the complaining customer to us as an adversary; in truth, such a customer is working to save the relationship. He or she is our greatest ally and we should value them as such.

Only one can be right, but both can win.

In my experience, it takes a fundamentall positive, customer-oriented attitude and a lo

[104] Reklamationsmanagement – Geschenke der Kunden (Peter Diehsle), aus „Erfolgsfakto Kundenzufriedenheit (Hansjörg Künzel, Springer Verlag Berlin Heidelberg, 2012)

[105] Mehr als ein Käufer: Der Kunde, das unbekannte Wesen (Lutz von Rosenstiel und Peter Neumann), aus „Erfolgsfaktor Kundenzufriedenheit (Hansjörg Künzel, Springer Verlag Berlin Heidelberg, 2012)

of empathy to successfully deal with conflict situations. In any case, instead of placing blame, shift the focus to solving problems. As the saying goes: *Only one can be right, but both can win.*

EMPATHY AS A KEY DIFFERENTIATOR

The perceived quality of a service is assessed from the customer's perspective, in terms of the price-performance ratio. As projects are social systems, we can't hope to understand what makes them tick unless we interact with our customers and feel genuinely interested in them. We shouldn't be spending time with our customers only when we want to sell something to them; we should be striving continuously to learn about them and their problems, their everyday lives, and their environment. This is the only way we can expect to create the necessary and fundamental understanding of our customers that forms the basis of a real partnership. The next time we meet our customers, we should put away our sales agendas and start to care for our customers in an empathetic way.

In our society, the notion of what it is to serve has accrued some negative connotations. There is a difference between servitude and stewardship. All too often, the consideration and empathy requisite for true stewardship are interpreted as signs of weakness[106]. We've all heard the saying "Whoever serves has not made it." Out of fear of being disrespected, one tries to remain the master of things and not to put oneself on the level of the weak—the servant. In a world full of high-performing managers, those who serve are often made to feel like underdogs, and this negative self-assessment drags them down. This is exactly how professional service will fail.

[106] Die Persönlichkeit macht den Unterschied (Jens Corssen), aus „Erfolgsfaktor Kundenzufriedenheit (Hansjörg Künzel, Springer Verlag Berlin Heidelberg, 2012)

In today's service society, an ever-increasing number of people require services. Yet who is truly prepared to serve? Who will enthusiastically meet this great demand? It is crucial to serve from a position of strength and dignity—instead of *I have to serve; I choose to serve.* Without this conscious decision to serve, it will hardly be possible to really be of service to the customer, to advise him, to provide him with the solutions to his problems, and to accompany him throughout a lifetime. Nevertheless, the customer is not king, but an equal partner.

The question remains: Why do we fail as service providers? To answer this, we must begin by engaging in personal dialogue with our customers to learn how they measure standards of quality, in order to derive competitive advantages. Then, we have to take a stance vis-à-vis our services and work out the competitive advantages. This cannot be a top-down management initiative as the lack of credibility would render it ineffective; instead, it must be driven bottom-up by every person who is in contact with our customers. We must build up the personalities of our employees in terms of their psychological and social competences so that they may truly connect with our customers and with each other. Doing so will fulfil our customers' demand for an optimised service experience. Furthermore, the interpersonal relationships between our employees and those of our customers will form a strong, lasting foundation that can't be imitated or replaced, which they will be thoroughly invested in and eager to maintain.

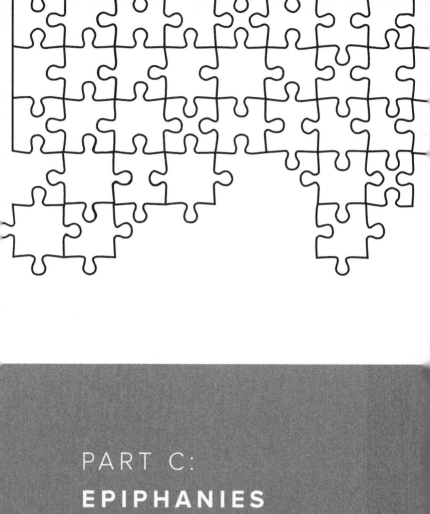

PART C:
EPIPHANIES

THE CHAPTERS IN THIS SECTION REVIEW the topics discussed in Part A to provide takeaway guides summarising key indicators and strategies.

It covers the essential strategies for the foundational work that needs to be done - changing yourself and your teams and organisations, and establishing and maintaining the various types of connections necessary to enact and support change. We also revisit three of our key players to see how they have fared and where they are today, to provide an idea of how some of these archetypal characters' strengths, limitations and working styles can play out within various dynamics.

I hope you'll take away these thoughts in whatever form you find most helpful.

13 | EVIL GUIDE TO CORPORATE SUCCESS

W E'VE ALL HEARD IT SAID THAT NICE GUYS FINISH LAST. I'VE encountered many people who conduct their entire careers according to this philosophy. We've even met a few of them already in Part A. I would refer to such individuals as operators. They are always looking out for number one and are willing to do whatever it takes to protect their position. They are happy to manipulate the system to get what they want.

While this may seem to work out well for them in the short term, their personal advancement often comes at the expense of the greater good. Their self-serving behaviour compromises the wellbeing of their projects, and this has a knock-on effect on the progress of the whole organisation. Ultimately, this will come back to haunt them, as the future of the organisation is their future as well.

I had some fun composing this chapter as a guide for how evil people fight their way to the top. As you'll see, it's really a guide for helping you to identify some of the toxic behaviours of such operators

tors, so that you can set them straight before they adversely impact your team and your whole organisation.

MY JOB IS DEFINED BY MY BUDGET, THE DURATION, AND THE PEOPLE INVOLVED.

Remember Carey? She's the person who always knows how to spin things. We could also call her The Successful Project Person. What are her secrets?

Here are Carey's tried and tested strategies for achieving corporate project success (for herself, at least):

1 | **Secure the budget**, and you will be safe for a long time to come. As soon as the opportunity presents itself, secure as much budget as you possibly can, as this gives you more flexibility for the project, automatically extends the duration of the project, and takes you past the point of no return. A project that has used up a certain amount of money is too big to fail. This guarantees job security for a long time to come. I worked on one project that had eighty developers working on its software project across five years. After four and a half years, a report showed that the project—its technology, in particular—was no longer suitable for practical use.

The project was discontinued, but all of the projects surrounding it were kept running. Why did it take them five years to realise that the project was a flop? Or were some people aware that it was doomed to fail? I don't know which of these is worse. When you learn that they had invested tens of millions of Euro into this project, it's easy to guess at the forces and logic that kept this turnip running.

This probably goes without saying, but never give up any budget you've already secured. Even if there is another project somewhere in the company that desperately needs it, that's not your problem.

They will figure something out. Never, ever give up any of your budget, for the reasons given above. This topic is addressed in a Harald Willenbrock article published in *brandeins*, in which Nick Jue, CEO of ING, has some fascinating insights to share about budgeting.[107] There may be subtle differences across industries, but the overall pattern is the same, so don't assume this applies only to banking.

2 | **Think only from milestone to milestone.** With every milestone you achieve, your organisation will come to trust you more. The longer it takes to complete these milestones, the less clear and defined they need to be. Keep in mind that, according to project management basics, milestones should not be moved. Therefore, as long as you don't define too many of them, you won't need to show real incremental results. Do not make them too precise, either. Let the theory work for you. Deflect questions by saying: *I have followed the theory to the letter, so there can't be any problems with project management.*

3 | **Cover your bases** by utilising all of the following tactics: create more hierarchies; appoint a scapegoat (e.g., Jessy Jetsetter, Homer Homebody, Dillon Disillusioned); hire consultants to whom you can later assign blame; introduce complexity and dependencies between projects

4 | **Build a team of trusted colleagues and trustees.** You are all in this together, working for the common cause towards collective success. The more minions you have, the better. The external company provides you with its available personnel. Whether or not these people represent the best talent remains to be

[107] Willenbrock, Harald. "Eine Bank auf Speed." Brand Eins. April 2018. https://bit.ly/2FVCanU

seen - you certainly can't be expected to individually screen them. You appoint your trusted advisors to oversee the external hires, and now the responsibility lies with them. Execute your strategy wisely. You cannot count on all of your cronies to remain loyal. As far as possible, you should occupy a seat of power and always be seeking to forge new alliances. You and your cohorts will navigate the big ship into the sphere of influence. You want the company's leadership to sit up and take notice, but not to the extent that they will demand too much of you or examine you closely. And when it comes to the crunch, you can blame your minions for anything that hasn't gone quite according to plan.

If you have done all of the above, you will remain in a protective cloud for a very long time. You will be safe from any accusations. The longer a project takes, the more certainty you'll have that things will be correctly done. You'll also have enough time to correct things later on, as there is not enough time right now to ensure quality, and so on.

The worst-case scenario is that the project will be discontinued, because it has been running for too long. Even if it is discontinued, you needn't worry. You have acquired so much knowledge and are so enmeshed in the process that you will be guaranteed a place in the next phase or initiative. You will have protected your position by broadcasting everything you've done right and blaming others for everything that went wrong.

The next phase is bound to be a success. Why is that? Well, we've already invested in so much effort into this. That's why it can't fail.

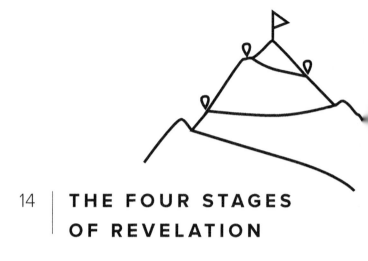

14 | THE FOUR STAGES OF REVELATION

Whenever I lead training sessions and workshops, the time can be broken down into four phases. These stages of revelation mimic typical corporate life as well. In one workshop session, we seem to move through the entire journey experienced during any client project.

In my sessions and workshops, I try to build an atmosphere of intimacy and honesty over a dedicated timeframe that allows enough time to see real change happening. The people involved need to be passionate about what has been started. As a result, change will be visible, perhaps not immediately, but it will shine through eventually. Let us have a look at how this unfolds.

PHASE ONE - ZERO EXPECTATION

The attendees enter the session, seeming curious and slightly sceptical about what is coming next. As my training sessions are internally provided by the company for whom they work, they may have been eagerly awaiting it, in which case they will have extremely high expectations; or they may have chosen it at random from the training calendar so that they can spend some time away from their project, in which case they will display a supreme lack of motivation. Their managers may have signed them up for this session.

In most cases, they are waiting to see what will happen and are not necessarily all that engaged.

I often have the pleasure of being introduced with a statement that goes something like this: *Welcome, everyone. I have requested your attendance, because I believe it to be necessary. All of you have to pass the mandatory exam at the end, and I expect you all to be fully engaged, now in the training as well as afterwards in your new roles. Please pay attention, so that we can look forward to a successful project.*

You can imagine their enthusiasm and engagement, as well as their openness in asking questions, especially when their managers remain in the training session with them. Nevertheless, they stand to learn quite a lot, as the managers usually do most of the talking and ask the questions that the employees are too terrified or reluctant to ask. At this time, I open the session by welcoming them and saying we are going to have an awesome time together.

PHASE TWO - THE UNCONSCIOUS MIND

Particularly when learning something that seems simple at first glance, the attendees wish to progress very quickly through those chapters. I present the training topics in terms of mindset, culture, principles, ways of thinking, intrinsic motivation, and looking at things from different angles. As these topics are not practically applicable, they may seem rather abstract for the time being. Whether they are there because they crave some life-altering revelation or have been forced to attend, attendees may start to grow impatient at this point, as I haven't provided them with any handy checklists or guidelines or confirmed something they already had in mind. In the best case, I'm depicting a perfect world that they believe has no relevance to their specific environment. They may feel that unless this session perfectly matches their demands and expectations, it isn't for them. As we work our way through these topics, we start to cover more topics that are new to them.

PHASE THREE - WILLFUL NEGLIGENCE

Now, we get into doing some practical stuff. This is where I usually come up against plenty of resistance, because many of the attendees don't see how these exercises will transfer to the real world. I think you can guess which of the attendees tend to be the most resistant. *I don't see any sense in playing with Lego when our work environment is so complex,* they say. *This makes sense in theory, but it won't work here.* Discussions arise, objections are voiced, applicability is questioned, and we often see a general reluctance to look at things from different angles. However, this is exactly the time when perspectives and attitudes undergo the biggest changes. You just have to make sure that some people don't spoil the experience for everyone. We see resistance coming from those in middle management, in particular, as they understand that their power of influence may soon come into question.

PHASE FOUR - A NEW DAWN

When we enter the final phase, it all begins to come together. The participants begin to understand and make use of various topics and ask questions that are more thoughtful, interesting and layered

If they have not already begun to do so during the earlier stages, the managers now take the lead in asking questions or even deconstructing earlier assumptions and preconceptions. At this point, people start to understand what all of this really means for them personally, what will change, and how specific responsibilities and aspects will impact each individual as well as the team as a whole.

Team leads fear the loss of control, in terms of no longer being the brightest person in the room and no longer having the last word. They dread having to ask for things, including information, instead of being the proxy for everything. Dismantling the status quo is often initiated by asking questions or making bold statements. *Now that we have seen the theory, let's see what we can apply in practice.* Or: *Of course, not everything will be possible in our company, but if we handpick some elements and combine them, that will be sufficient.* These people may be the ones who have offered their colleagues something new and inspiring, while holding onto certain responsibilities and aspects that they claim are crucial to the company.

15 | **ESSENTIAL
STRATEGIES**

THIS BOOK IS ABOUT PEOPLE LIKE YOU AND ME. WE WORK WITH companies and individuals who are trying to make our world a better place with the products or services they provide. We go out into the field to work primarily with teams of people, so we need to be able to get along with various characters and to help individuals of all personality types to collaborate harmoniously and work together to change the world.

Our work involves different kinds of connections, because successful, sustained change can only happen when the connections are all intact, because that's when the communication flows. We need to be in touch with ourselves first of all, before we can connect with others; and we need to connect with people on an individual level and at the team and organisational levels, to help them connect with each other. Finally, we help these companies and the individuals working within them to connect with their customers through the products and services they provide. Here is a quick review of essential strategies for establishing and nurturing these connections to channel change.

CONNECTING WITH YOURSELF

Change starts within the self. Review what you have learned so far. Look back through your notes. Skim the chapters you've already read and re-read any sections that have resonated with you.

Make some notes as you reflect on the following topics:

- Your personal motivation, goals, and career ambitions
- Any personal feedback you've received about the above topics
- The roles you already play within your team, your organisation and your personal life; the roles you would like to take on; and the roles you are afraid to take on
- The structure of your organisation (including how well it accommodates the workflows, and whether it is an Agile environment)

Unless we truly come to know and understand ourselves, we can't expect to know and understand others to the extent that we can help them to change. Here are some strategies and rubrics for learning more about yourself.

- Take some personality and psychometric tests and learn about your personality type. Useful tests include:
  - ☑ Myers-Briggs Type Indicator
  - ☑ 16Personalities (www.16personalities.com)
  - ☑ DISC profile

- Seek regular feedback from people who know you in various capacities, including:
  - ☑ colleagues and supervisors at work
  - ☑ close friends
  - ☑ peers within other environments, e.g. teams and clubs

- Try out some new ways to relax and connect with yourself:
  - ☑ meditation or yoga
  - ☑ taking part in sports or watching live sports
  - ☑ playing or listening to music
  - ☑ nature walks or camping outdoors

- Consider the roles you play, especially in terms of how and why they suit you, and whether you see any contradictions between them. These might include:
  - ☑ personal: parent, friend, partner, confidant
  - ☑ corporate: coach, employee, supervisor, leader
  - ☑ leisure: trainer, teammate, creator, learner

- Discover your ikigai. You may find it helpful to reflect upon your ambitions and drivers, as well as your barriers and nemeses, and ask yourself the following questions:
  - ☑ What makes you happy?
  - ☑ How do you recharge your energy?
  - ☑ What or who drains your energy?
  - ☑ What is important to you?
  - ☑ What are your goals?
  - ☑ What are your strengths?
  - ☑ What things do you like about yourself?
  - ☑ What do you dislike about yourself?

CONNECTING WITH OTHER PEOPLE

Before you can lead and guide other people through real change you have to understand where they are coming from and what they need and want, so you can effectively communicate and connec with them.

- Learn about what motivates other people, using various references and tools, including:
  - ☑ Moving Motivators cards
  - ☑ Researching personality types

- Learn about empathy and emotional intelligence
  - ☑ Read this article about why understanding other people's perspectives is a key leadership skill.[108]

- Develop your powers of observation and listening skills
  - ☑ Practice active listening
  - ☑ "Most people do not listen with the intent to understand; they listen with the intent to reply."[109]

- Learn about building trust. You can start with the following resources:
  - ☑ Refer to the trust equation to measure how much you trust other people and how much they trust you
  - ☑ Read *The Trusted Advisor*[110] and *Speed of Trust*[111]

CONNECTING WITH TEAMS

In order to optimise the progress and performance of an organisation and the teams within it, you have to be able to connect with them and help them to connect with each other. Here are some essential

[108] Surdek, Steffan. "Why Understanding Other Perspectives Is A Key Leadership Skill" Forbes. Accessed 27 September 2020. https://bit.ly/3mQxnFf

[109] Covey, Stephen M.R.. *The 7 Habits of Highly Effective People.* Simon + Schuster, 2004.

[110] Maister, David, Green Charles H. & Robert M. Galford. *The Trusted Advisor.* Free Press, 2000.

[111] Covey, Stephen M.R.. The Speed of Trust: The One Thing that Changes Everything. Simon + Schuster, 2008

strategies to understand what makes them tick, how group dynamics work, and what unifies them in pursuing their targets so that you can guide them to communicate and collaborate more effectively.

- Apply the Tuckman team building model,[112] which consists of 5 elemental phases: forming, storming, norming, performing, adjourning
- Mobilise your team using the Team Canvas,[113] specifying purpose, team rules, mission, values, how success is defined
- Learn about the nine essential team roles, known as Belbin team roles[114]
- Conduct reflective feedback sessions together and approach learning as a team effort
- Encourage openness and feedback. Some ways to engender a nurturing and constructive learning environment include:
  - ☑ Encourage team members to express divergent views without fear, and to see that conflict can be healthy
  - ☑ Undertake training for giving and receiving feedback

CONNECTING COMPANIES WITH THEIR CUSTOMERS

The next step is to help organisations to connect with their customers by showing them how to listen to their customers and understand what they really need, and how to guide their teams to work in alignment with the organisation's structure and processes towards a clear mission and a shared vision to build truly great products or services.

---

[112] "5 Stages of a Team Development Tuckman", ProjectPM.
Accessed 27 September 2020. https://bit.ly/337yeJS

[113] "10 Scientifically Proven Ways to Build and Manage Great Teams", INC.
Accessed 27 September 2020. https://bit.ly/3i4ttoF

[114] "The Nine Belbin Team Roles." Belbin. Accessed 24 July 2020. https://bit.ly/2Fprai9

- Know what makes a product in the sweet spot[115]
- Learn to understand your customer using tools from product development as jobs-to-be-done, personae, journey maps, empathy maps
- Stay informed about what latest technology offers, get the IT department on board, and leverage IT appropriately
- Form cross-functional or interdisciplinary teams[116] that create world's best features

CONNECTING WITH ORGANISATIONS

I would suggest checking out *Leading Change[117]* by John Kotter. His eight-step process provides useful guidelines for steering a successful change initiative. You can even use it as a checklist.

You start by proving that there is a need for change and that this need is pressing. You form a core coalition to drive the process with you, and together you create a targeted vision that is inspiring, valuable and desirable. Then you extend your radius of influence by connecting with other likeminded individuals in various departments and at all levels of your organisation. You earn their support by proving your value and the value of the recommended change, and by fielding their questions and addressing their concerns, thus removing doubt, fear, and other barriers. While providing any guidance and support they need, you make a step forward and generate the first wins. Market these wins to further prove that making the recommended change will pay off and that the value benefit outweighs the effort.

---

[115] "Surviving and Thriving in an emerging Digital Media World: 4 Secrets to Success" DigitalHunters. Accessed 27 September. https://bit.ly/2G4ePAH

[116] "Feature Teams." Feature Teams. Accessed 29 Aug. 2020 https://featureteams.org/

[117] Kotter, John. Leading Change. Harvard Business Review Press, 2012.

Real change takes time. Be patient while people are letting go of their old habits and ingrained patterns and adapting to the change. The aftercare is just as important as the process. Don't declare victory too early, as this may lead to complacency. Keep racking up the wins. Sustain and solidify the achievements.

There is no failsafe method for successfully driving change. Be willing to experiment with different methods and keep tweaking them until you find something that works for the environment and situation at hand. Be prepared to walk down a path of trial and error. I recommend the lean change management approach,[118] which entails short cycles lasting four to eight weeks each. During each cycle, you make a plan, roll it out, check what happened, and decide how to act upon these results. This is known as the PDCA (plan, do, check, act) cycle.[119] Utilising participative methods will help to engage, inspire and bond the people you are taking along on this journey.

Invest in a playground in which to try out and evaluate new ideas, with limited yet sufficient freedom. Work with user surveys early prototypes (e.g., sketches, paper models) and minimum viable features (MVFs). Referring to Eric Ries' Lean Startup methodology, first define a product-market fit, then carry out a Build it – Measure it – Learn feedback loop.[120]

- Keep up employee engagement, e.g., by using the essential 12 questions from the Gallup Survey[121]
- Get familiar with the elements of Agile organisations. You can

[118] "The Pomodoro Technique: Do More and Have Fun with Time Management." Franceso Cirillo (website). Accessed 24 July 2020. https://bit.ly/30WS4q6

[119] "PDCA." Wikipedia. Accessed 24 July 2020. https://en.wikipedia.org/wiki/PDCA

[120] Playford, Brendan. "9 Challenges Hindering Innovation in Your Organization." Decipher™ 9 June 2016. https://bit.ly/3mIYaDi

[121] "The 12 Questions from the Gallup Q12 Employee Engagement Survey." Social Reacher. Accessed 24 July 2020. https://bit.ly/343GWJK

start by learning about Agile frameworks or the crucial five trademarks.[122]

- In customer-oriented and time-to-market optimised organisations, flow of work should go throughout end-to-end customer-triggered value streams[123] to avoid the dependencies of typical functional silos

- Learn about modern and experimental forms of organisational structures such as network organisations[124] and the connected company.[125]

[122] "The five trademarks of agile organizations" McKinsey. Accessed 27 September. https://mck.co/369YLb9

[123] "Identify Value Streams and ARTs." SAFe: Scaled Agile® Last updated 28 September 2019. https://bit.ly/2GfMMxO

[124] "Network-centric organization." Wikipedia. Last modified 30 April 2020. https://bit.ly/3g1x45A

[125] Gray, David. "The Connected Company". Wordpress. 27 September 2020. https://bit.ly/30tR2RV

16 | **THE FUTURE LOOKS BRIGHT**

HAVING MADE IT THROUGH COUNTLESS STORIES OF DESPAIR existential angst, and chaos, perhaps finding yourself wincing (and chuckling, at times) in recognition, I hope you feel you've gained some new insight and a fresh perspective and that you're feeling less alone. I hope you're feeling excited and inspired to try out some of the methods we've discussed. Also the characters from our stories developed themselves - some voluntarily, some more compulsory. We share three of their stories that could have been written by life.

WHERE ARE THEY NOW?

After we last saw Bonny, her career path took some unexpected turns. She continued to ascend the company hierarchy. All the while, upper management continued to prioritise financial outcomes above investing in new ideas and talent. Shortly after she finally made it into the inner circle, the company was forced to declare bankruptcy

By this time, she was suffering from burnout and struggling with self-doubt.

Bonny started over in a small company with her only ambition being to keep her head above water. She didn't have the energy to fight, and she let go of the need to control everything. She began to observe others and listen to what they were saying. Her new work environment was healthy and supportive, and her colleagues were collaborative and driven. She was amazed to see that her more humancentric approach encouraged a higher level of engagement and commitment from her teams.

Over the next two years, Bonny gained a renewed sense of ambition and a different skillset. She then took over the strategic department of a big consulting company. In her new role, she seamlessly combined her former personae of pushy, output-focussed boss with her newly acquired people skills. She says she is enjoying the financial rewards as well as a level of fulfilment she has never experienced before.

Mickey is fairly close with Tom, a member of the administrative board. The two of them came up together in the company and have had a longstanding personal friendship and a good working relationship. Some time ago, after years of hearing Mickey complain about his rebellious, know-it-all subordinates, Tom suggested that they try something new. Mickey agreed without giving it too much thought. Tom sent over one of his new team leads, a millennial called Neville with an autonomous working style, ease of communication and altruistic outlook that would make this world a better place. He was supposed to work in Mickey's department for a designated period of four months. Though Mickey was somewhat sceptical of the plan, he has always trusted Tom. Tom conducted "Neville's mission" and "setting the scene" meetings with the two of them to get them started on the right track.

Neville served as Mickey's right hand and dealt with matters on his behalf, involving Mickey only where necessary. Neville set up an efficient mode of interaction with the team members and quickly learned about them and their area, drew upon their extensive knowledge, and listened to what they told him about their observations and needs. Employee satisfaction soared. At first it wasn't clear to everyone that Mickey wasn't that involved in these developments, so people from all over the department addressed their appreciative feedback to him. Having become curious about Neville, Mickey increased contact with him. Gradually, their interaction grew. Thanks to the lightweight structures and exchanges Neville had established, the department became a rising star. Neville assumed more responsibilities and enjoyed ever-greater latitude.

When the four months was up, Neville was asked to remain and take over the action area in Mickey's department, which was volatile, unpredictable, and chaotic and contained a lot of future topics Neville benefited from Mickey's network and his knowledge of the company and functional domain. The last we heard was that Mickey has taken over the steadier environment, which has incorporated a new mindset and practices in the meantime, and Neville has managed to extend the action area to create an unexpected new growth area in the company. The two have remained friends. Mickey will be the first to admit that quite some time ago it stopped being clear who is coaching whom. He says they both have found exactly what they were searching for.

Dillon's big news is that the company where he works underwent an Agile transformation. The day came when Dillon found himself in a Scrum team. How I would have loved to see it. By this time, he had already attended numerous training sessions an had acquired a lot of new skills. External coaches had introduced him to a brand new world, one in which he would seize the opportunity to speak up whenever he saw room for improvement, pull work from a task list based on his individual skills, and contribute his knowledge towards shaping goals. Like many others on the team, Dillon felt unsure of the situation. But these new leads, who called themselves the Scrum Master and the Product Owner, did a really good job. They involved the team, checked with everyone on competencies and content-related knowledge, and acted on what they said. They challenged the team in a friendly manner. Dillon's apathy melted away and he reverted to his curious and enthusiastic younger self. He became more interested in learning new things and sharing his ideas. As one of the more senior members within the Scrum team, he even took over a lead role for developing a new topic. As all this was taking place at a sustainable pace (within usual office hours), Dillon didn't feel that it posed any threat to any of the things that have become so important to him. So much has changed in Dillon's world. If you were to meet his team today, you wouldn't even recognise him.

WHAT DOES THE FUTURE HOLD?

Over the years, I've encountered so many organisations and individuals. While each of them is unique and every encounter is different, there are three things that always come to the surface to restore my faith in the future. I hope they will remain with you after reading this book:

People get it.

They know what it is all about. Sometimes it takes time for them to let go or to process the information, but with every passing moment, it makes more sense.

People learn.

They are eager to apply this newly acquired knowledge to their environment, but the organisation tries to confine them to known territory, with no possibility of trying something new.

Telling stories does work.

While change always enacts the same phases, it is stories that bring understanding. Stories do not provide solutions; they allow us to build a wealth of references, knowledge and experience, positioning us to form our own solutions. From what I have seen, it isn't possible to provide a set of easy answers, as the questions will always vary in subtle yet significant ways. It is far more helpful to share a range of situations, perspectives and outcomes, thus equipping people to draw their own conclusions.

AFTERWORD

THE MORE PEOPLE KNOW ABOUT WHAT REALLY HAPPENS WITHin corporations, the sooner they will understand that something needs to change. Perhaps we need to create more awareness by opening a dialogue and sharing our stories. If you are aware of all the things that can happen, all of the motivation and enthusiasm you feel when embarking upon a new project or starting a new job could be properly harnessed and unleash its full potential. If you don't know what to expect, you might encounter these obstacles and become disillusioned, demoralised and disenfranchised. You may start to think, as so many people do: *No one understands where I am coming from. So many people are doing things differently—perhaps I am doing something wrong. I might as well keep swimming with the current. Let someone else save the world. I'll just make it easy on myself.*

I believe that we are all fighters. It's not in our true nature to give up. If we truly believe in something, if we think we can help, it's worth it to us to try, regardless of the hardship we might have to endure. Don't be afraid of going against the tide. Once we master the tides, they can bring us wherever we want to go. As long as we know what to expect out there, and come equipped with the necessary knowledge and skills, we can have a great ride. It might be rough at times. There will be bad moments and better moments. But we will get better with every passing day and we'll have fun while we're at it.

AUTHOR'S NOTE

Thank you for coming on this journey with me. If you loved the book and have a minute to spare, it would mean a lot to us if you could post a short review on Goodreads, Amazon or any other fine review sites.

Reviews from readers like you make a huge difference to authors. Help us to spread the word about solving #TheRiddleOfChangeInOrganisations.

Direct link to the book's Amazon Review page:

Thank you!
Henrik Gruber and Alexander Birke

P.S. If you'd like to receive occasional updates, you can sign up for the newsletter here:
http://www.stumblingacrosstheobvious.com/

APPENDIX

ACKNOWLEDGEMENTS

Fᴵʳˢᵗ ᴀɴᴅ ꜰᴏʀᴇᴍᴏꜱᴛ, ɪ'ᴅ ʟɪᴋᴇ ᴛᴏ ᴛʜᴀɴᴋ ᴍʏ ᴡɪꜰᴇ ᴊᴜʟɪᴀ, ᴡɪᴛʜ-out whom this book would not exist.

I'm grateful to Alexander Birke for his generous and wise contributions to this book. My heartfelt thanks to all guest writers for providing fresh perspectives and valuable insights from a different profession.

Thanks to Mirko Hering for guiding me through the publishing jungle. Thank you, Kate Agramonte, Martin Lehner, Friederike Breucker, and Jan Bruckner, for your valuable feedback.

I'd like to thank my research assistant and the book's interior designer. And I'm very grateful to my editor.

Special thanks to Lisa Berndorfer for her design advice. I owe a debt of gratitude to all of my clients, for entrusting me with their projects and for the enlightening experiences we've shared.

Finally, I'd like to thank you, the reader. I hope to hear from you, so that I can learn from you too.

Thank you all.

HENRIK GRUBER

EMAIL
Henrik.gruber@pm.me

LINKEDIN
www.linkedin.com/in/henrik-gruber

ALEXANDER BIRKE

EMAIL
Alexander.birke@gmail.com

LINKEDIN
www.linkedin.com/in/alexbirke-businessagility

www.stumblingacrosstheobvious.com

GLOSSARY

ADKAR   An acronym which stands for Awareness, Desire, Knowledge, Ability and Reinforcement. It explains that the process of becoming ready for change is sequential, starting from the current level of each individual and none of the five steps can be skipped.

Agile frameworks   Agile was popularised by the Manifesto for Agile Software Development. The values and principles espoused in this manifesto were derived from and underpin a broad range of software development frameworks, including Scrum and Scaled Agile frameworks.

Agile Release Train (ART)   The Agile Release Train (ART) is a collective of Agile teams, which, along with other stakeholders, incrementally develops, delivers, and where applicable operates, one or more products.

Community of Practise (CoP)   A group of people who share a concern or a passion for something they do and learn how to do it better as they interact regularly.

Conway's law   An adage stating that organisations design systems that mirror their own communication structure. It is named after computer programmer Melvin Conway, who introduced the idea in 1967.

Critical Chain Method   Critical chain project management (CCPM) is a method of planning and managing projects that emphasizes the resources (people, equipment, physical space) required to execute project tasks. It was developed by Eliyahu M. Goldratt. A critical chain project network strives to keep resources levelled, and requires that they be flexible in start times.

Customer journey   A customer journey map shows the story of the customer's experience. It not only identifies key interactions that the customer has with the organization, but it also brings user's feelings, motivations and questions for each of the touchpoints. Finally, a customer journey map has the objective of teaching organizations more about their customers.

Daily stand-ups   Meetings in which attendees typically participate while standing. The discomfort of standing for long periods is intended to keep the meetings short.

Delegation Poker   A card game designed by Jurgen Appelo to help people and teams to agree on a level of delegation for key decision areas. The ensuing discussion fosters mutual understanding and empathy.

Design Thinking   The cognitive, strategic and practical processes by which design concepts (such as proposals for new products, buildings, machines, etc.) are developed. Many of the key concepts and aspects of design thinking have been identified through studies, across different design domains, of design cognition and design activity in both laboratory and natural contexts.

DISC Assessment   A behaviour assessment tool developed by industrial psychologist Walter Vernon Clarke, based on psychologist William Moulton Marston's DISC theory, which centres on four key personality traits: dominance, influence, steadiness, and conscientiousness.

Eisenhower Matrix   The "Eisenhower Method" stems from a quote attributed to Dwight D. Eisenhower: "I have two kinds of problems, the urgent and the important. The urgent are not important, and the important are never urgent."

End-to-End (E2E)   Used to describe a process that takes a system or a service from beginning to end and delivers a complete functional solution, usually without needing to obtain anything from a third party.

Flight Levels   The various levels of detail for visualising work. Level consists of a team level view up to level 3 which show the company portfolio.

Flow Management

Lean Flow is about how items or people in a process move from the first step to the last. The intention in Lean flow is to move the item or product through the process as quick as possible, without any risk to quality and customer satisfaction.

Getting Things Done (GTD)

A method for moving planned tasks and projects out of the mind by recording them externally and then breaking them into actionable work items. This allows attention to be focused on taking action on tasks instead of recalling them.

Ikigai

Ikigai (生き甲斐) is a Japanese concept that means "a reason for being". A direction or purpose in life that makes one's life meaningful.

Impediments

A hindrance or obstruction in doing something. Within projects often referred to within the realm of improvements.

Intent-based leadership

Intent-Based Leadership™ is fundamentally the language leaders and teams use to communicate at work – the words we use with each other and how we ask questions – in order to give control to people, so people who are closest to the information are the ones making the decisions.

Kanban

Kanban (看板), which literally translates as signboard or billboard, is a scheduling system for lean manufacturing and just-in-time manufacturing (JIT). Taiichi Ohno, an industrial engineer at Toyota, developed kanban to improve manufacturing efficiency. The system takes its name from the cards that track production within a factory.

KPI

A key performance indicator (KPI) is a type of performance measurement. KPIs evaluate the success of an organisation or of a particular activity (e.g., a project, program, product or initiative) in which it engages.

Kübler-Ross Change Curve

A model consisting of the five stages of emotion experienced by a person who is approaching death or is grieving the death of a loved one. The phases are defined as denial, anger, bargaining, depression and acceptance.

Large Scale Scrum (LeSS)

A framework for scaling Scrum to multiple teams who work together on a single product. It starts with a foundation of one Scrum team, and applies to multiple teams who work together on one product.

Lean Change Canvas

The Lean Change Canvas relates the typical canvas elements to an organisational change context. It maps each canvas element to one of Kotter's leading steps, identifies three risk classes, and proposes a certain work order for the quadrants.

Lean Techniques

Lean management is one of the top tools that eliminate waste in any process. Lean techniques are typically used in a production environment.

Magic Estimation / Affinity Estimation

Magic Estimation is an estimation technique that is quick. It is especially useful to quickly estimate a large number of items. The benefits of Magic Estimation are the speed (due to only non-verbal communication) and the subjectivity with which each team member can look at the process.

Maslow's hierarchy of needs

A motivational theory in psychology comprising a five-tiered model of human needs, often depicted as hierarchical levels within a pyramid. Needs lower down in the hierarchy must be satisfied before individuals can attend to needs higher up. In order of importance, the needs are defined as physiological, safety, love and belonging, esteem, and self-actualisation.

McKinsey 7S Framework

A strategic vision for groups (e.g., businesses, business units, and teams). The elements are defined as structure, strategy, systems, skills, style, staff, and shared values. The model is most often used as an organisational analysis tool to assess and monitor changes in the internal situation of an organisation.

Minimum viable feature (MVF)

A small-scale feature that can quickly be built and rolled out (using minimal resources) to a target population to test the feature's usefulness and adoption.

Minimum viable product (MVP) A product with enough features to attract early-adopter customers and validate a product idea early in the product development cycle. In industries such as software, the MVP can help the product team receive user feedback as quickly as possible to iterate and improve the product.

Moving Motivators An exercise designed by Jurgen Appelo to help to reflect on the ten intrinsic motivating desires and how they affect organisational change. Inspired by the work of Daniel Pink, Steven Reiss, and Edward Deci.

Myers-Briggs Type Indicator MBTI A self-report questionnaire indicating differing psychological preferences in how people perceive the world and make decisions.

North Star vision A clear and powerful mission statement.

Obeya A component of lean manufacturing, obeya (大部屋), which translates as "great room", originated in the 1990s at Toyota during the conception of the Prius. All key personnel engaged on a project meet in one room to facilitate communication and reduce department thinking. The obeya has been likened to the bridge of a ship, a war room, and a brain.

Objectives and key results (OKR) A goal-setting framework for defining and tracking objectives and their outcomes.

Plan, Do, Check, Act (PDCA) An iterative four-step management method used in business for the control and continuous improvement of processes and products. It is also known as the Deming circle/cycle/wheel, the Shewhart cycle, the control circle/cycle, or plan–do–study–act (PDSA).

Pomodoro Technique A time management method developed by Francesco Cirillo in the late 1980s. The technique uses a timer to break down work into intervals, traditionally 25 minutes in length, separated by short breaks.

Project Management Institute (PMI)	The world's leading project management organisation, with over 600,000 global members and over 300 local chapters.
Refactoring	The process of restructuring existing computer code, changing the factoring, without changing its external behaviour. Refactoring is intended to improve the design, structure, and/or implementation of the software (its non-functional attributes), while preserving its functionality.
Satir Change Model	A transformation system developed by family therapist Virginia Satir to people improve their lives by transforming the way they see and express themselves.
Scaled Agile Framework (SAFe)	A set of organisation and workflow patterns intended to guide enterprises in scaling lean and agile practices One of a growing number of frameworks that seek to address the problems encountered when scaling beyond a single team.
Scrum	Scrum is an Agile framework for developing, delivering and sustaining complex products.
Taylorism (Frederick Taylor)	Scientific management is a theory of management that analyses and synthesises workflows. Its main objectiv is improving economic efficiency, especially labour productivity.
Truck factor	The number of people on a team who would have to be hit with a truck before the project would be in serious trouble.
Value stream	An end-to-end collection of value-adding activitie that create an overall result for a customer, stakeholde or end-user.
Work in Progress (WIP) limits	The maximum number of task items in the various stage of the workflow. Limiting the number of works in progress is one of the core properties of Kanban.

BIBLIOGRAPHY

"5 Reasons Why Customers Don't Want to Wait on Hold." VHT Marketing. Accessed 29 August 2020. https://vhtcx.com/blog/5-reasons-why-customers-dont-want-to-wait-on-hold/

"5 Stages of a Team Development Tuckman", ProjectPM. Accessed 27 September 2020.https://project.pm/team-development-tuckman/

"7 Wastes of Lean: How to Optimize Resources." Kanbanize. Accessed 27 July 2020. https://kanbanize.com/lean-management/value-waste/7-wastes-of-lean

"10 Scientifically Proven Ways to Build and Manage Great Teams", INC. Accessed 27 September 2020. https://www.inc.com/jeff-haden/10-scientifically-proven-ways-to-buildand-manage-great-teams-wed.html

"The 12 Questions from the Gallup Q12 Employee Engagement Survey." Social Reacher. Accessed 24 July 2020. https://socialreacher.com/blog/the-12-questions-from-the-gallup-q12-employee-engagement-survey/

"20 Questions to Ask Customers about Your Product." User Testing. Accessed 29 August 2020. https://www.usertesting.com/blog/20-questions-every-product-manager-should-ask

"Affinity Estimating: A HOW-TO" GettingAgile. Accessed 11 Oct. 2020. https://www.gettingagile.com/2008/07/04/affinity-estimating-a-how-to/

"Ageing and Employment Policies: Statistics on average effective age of retirement." OECD. Accessed 16 June 2020. https://www.oecd.org/els/emp/average-effective-age-of-retirement.htm

Appelo, Jurgen. "The 7 Levels of Delegation." *Medium*. 25 Feb. 2015. https://medium.com/@jurgenappelo/the-7-levels-of-delegation-672ec2a48103

Appelo, Jurgen. *Management 3.0: Leading Agile Developers, Developing Agile Leaders*. Addison-Wesley Professional, 2011.

Arruda, William. "Nine Differences Between Being a Leader and a Manager." Forbes. 15 Nov. 2016. https://www.forbes.com/sites/williamarruda/2016/11/15/9-differences-between-being-a-leader-and-a-manager/#3c89d2964609

Ashkenas, Ron. "Your Career Needs to Be Horizontal." *Ascend* (blog). *Harvard Business Review*. 7 July 2019. https://hbrascend.org/topics/career-needs-horizontal/

Bailey, Dave. "How to Deliver Constructive Feedback in Difficult Situations." Medium. 8 April 2019 https://medium.com/s/please-advise/the-essential-guide-to-difficult-conversations-41f736e63ccf

Baker, Tim. "Is It Time to Kill the Job Description?" 27 February 2017. *HRM*. https://www.hrmonline.com.au/section/strategic-hr/time-kill-job-description/

Biech, Elaine. "Why Is Training Necessary?" *Dummies*. Accessed 28 July 2020 https://www.dummies.com/business/human-resources/employee-engagement/why-is-training-necessary/

Blank, Steve. "Hacking a Corporate Culture: Stories, Heroes, and Rituals in Startups and Companies." 9 September 2015. https://steveblank.com/2015/09/09/hacking-a-corporate-culture-stories-heroes-and-rituals-in-startups-and-companies/

Bloch, Michael, Sven Blumberg, and Jürgen Laartz. "Delivering large-scale IT projects on time, on budget, and on value." 1 October 2012. *McKinsey Digital*. Accessed 27 July 2020. https://www.mckinsey.com/business-functions/mckinsey-digital/our-insights/delivering-large-scale-it-projects-on-time-on-budget-and-on-value#

Bowler, Michael. "Truck Factor." 15 May 2005. http://www.agileadvice.com/2005/05/15/agilemanagement/truck-factor/

Bowman, Sharon. *Training from the Back of the Room: 65 Ways to Step Aside and Let Them Learn*. Pfeiffer, Dec. 2008.

Brooks, Fred. *Mythical Man Month: Essays on Software Engineering*. Addison-Wesley, 1975.

Butler, Patrick. "No Grammar School, Lots of Play: The Secrets of Europe's Top Education System." *The Guardian* online. 20 Sept. 2016. https://www.theguardian.com/education/2016/sep/20/grammar-schools-play-europe-top-education-system-finland-daycare

Christensen, Clayton M., Michael E. Raynor, and Rory McDonald. "What Is Disruptive Innovation?" *Harvard Business Review*. From Dec. 2015 issue https://hbr.org/2015/12/what-is-disruptive-innovation

Ciccotti, Kevin. "The Human Factor in Project Management." Paper presented at PMI® Global Congress 2014—North America, Phoenix, AZ. Newtown Square, PA: Project Management Institute. https://www.pmi.org/learning/library/human-factor-project-management-9276

"Consultants." United Nations Development Programme. Accessed 28 Jun 2020. https://www.undp.org/content/undp/en/home/jobs/types-of-opportunities/consultants-individual-contractors.html

Covey, Stephen M.R.. The 7 Habits of Highly Effective People. Simon + Schuster, 2004.

Covey, Stephen M.R.. The Speed of Trust: The One Thing that Changes Everything. Simon +Schuster, 2008

Craveiro, João. "Marty Meets Martin: Connecting the Two Triads of Product Development." Medium. 18 Nov. 2017. https://productcoalition.com/marty-meets-martin-connecting-the-two-triads-of-product-management-5c7cb2c9004f

"Create a New Lean Change Canvas." Canvanizer. Accessed 29 Aug. 2020. https://canvanizer.com/new/lean-change-canvas

"Create a New Lean Change Canvas." Canvanizer. Accessed 29 Aug. 2020. https://canvanizer.com/new/lean-change-canvas

"Creating a Culture of Innovation: Focus on These 3 Factors." Center for Creative Leadership. Accessed 29 Aug. 2020 https://www.ccl.org/articles/leading-effectively-articles/8-factors-that-drive-or-suppress-innovation/

Crowther, Linnea. "The Five Stages of Grief." 19 February 2019. Legacy.com. https://www.legacy.com/advice/the-five-stages-of-grief/

Csikszentmihalyi, Flow: The Psychology of Optimal Experience. Harper Perennial Modern Classics, 2008.

Cynefin framework." Wikipedia. Last modified 2 Sept. 2020. https://en.wikipedia.org/wiki/Cynefin_framework

"David Marquet: Intent-Based Leadership." The ArmyLeader.co.uk. Accessed 27 July 2020. https://thearmyleader.co.uk/david-marquet-intent-based-leadership/

"Delegation Poker & Delegation Board." Management 3.0. Accessed 29 Aug. 2020. https://management30.com/practice/delegation-poker/

Deming, W. Edwards. The New Economics for Industry, Government, Education. MIT Press,2000.

De Meyere, Annelies. "Change Management Canvases: The Hidden Power of the Storytelling Canvas." 14 March 2018. Co-Learning. https://co-learning.be/2018/03/14/change-management-canvases-the-hidden-power-of-the-story-telling-canvas/

Desjardins, Jess. "Every Single Cognitive Bias in One Infographic." Visual Capitalist. 25 Sept. 2017 https://www.visualcapitalist.com/every-single-cognitive-bias/

De Smet, Aaron, Gerald Lackey, Leigh M. Weiss. "Untangling your organization's decision making." 17 June 2017. *McKinsey Quarterly.* McKinsey & Company.

Die Persönlichkeit macht den Unterschied (Jens Corssen), aus „Erfolgsfaktor Kundenzufriedenheit (Hansjörg Künzel, Springer Verlag Berlin Heidelberg, 2012)

"DISC Personality Assessment." ©Truity. Accessed 24 July 2020. https://www.truity.com/test/disc-personality-test

"Dreyfus Model of Skill Acquisition." Wikipedia. Last modified 18 June 2020. https://en.wikipedia.org/wiki/Dreyfus_model_of_skill_acquisition

Dweck, Carol. "What Having a 'Growth Mindset' Actually Means." 13 January 2016. *Harvard Business Review.* https://hbr.org/2016/01/what-having-a-growth-mindset-actually-means

Dwyer, Christopher. "12 Common Biases that Affect How We Make Everyday Decisions." 7 Sept. 2018. *Psychology Today.* https://www.psychologytoday.com/us/blog/thoughts-thinking/201809/12-common-biases-affect-how-we-make-everyday-decisions

Elleithy, Salah. "Training from the BACK of the Room." Slide Share. 17 Dec 2014. [Slides] https://de.slideshare.net/sparkagility/training-from-the-back-of-the-room

"Feature Teams." Feature Teams. Accessed 29 Aug. 2020 https://featureteams.org/

Ferris, Tim. *Tools of Titans: The Tactics, Routines, and Habits of Billionaires, Icon and World-Class.* Vermilion, 2016

Fishbane, Monica. "Why Change is So Hard: The Power of Habit in the Human Brain." Good Therapy. https://www.goodtherapy.org/blog/why-change-is-so-hard-the-power-of-habit-in-the-human-brain-0317155

"The five trademarks of agile organizations" McKinsey. Accessed 27 September https://www.mckinsey.com/business-functions/organization/our-insights/the-fivetrademarks-of-agile-organizations

"Five Whys." Wikipedia. Last modified 15 Sept. 2020. https://en.wikipedia.org/wiki/Five_whys

"Frederick Taylor and Scientific Management: Understanding Taylorism and Early Management Theory." *Mind Tools* (website). Accessed 28 June 2020. https://www.mindtools.com/pages/article/newTMM_Taylor.htm

García, Héctor. *Ikigai: The Japanese Secret to a Long and Happy Life*. Penguin, 2017.

Gladwell, Malcolm. "Good Old Boys." Season 4, Episode 4. *Revisionist History* [podcast] Accessed 18 August 2020. http://revisionisthistory.com/episodes/34-good-old-boys

Gray, David. "The Connected Company". Wordpress. 27 September 2020. https://frankdiana.files.wordpress.com/2010/11/the-connected-company.pdf

Gulati, Ranjay and James B. Oldroyd. "The Quest for Customer Focus." *Harvard Business Review* (website). From the April 2005 issue. https://hbr.org/2005/04/the-quest-for-customer-focus

Hall, John. "10 Barriers to Employee Innovation." *Forbes*. 29 April 2013. https://www.forbes.com/sites/johnhall/2013/04/29/10-barriers-to-employee-innovation/#51c1a3b8117d

Hamel, Gary. "First, Let's Fire All the Managers." *Harvard Business Review*. From the Dec. 2011 issue. https://hbr.org/2011/12/first-lets-fire-all-the-managers

Heylighen, F. "The Problem of Suboptimisation." Modified 26 January 1999. Principia Cybernetica Web. http://pespmc1.vub.ac.be/SUBOPTIM.html

"IDEO's Human-Centered Design Process: How to Make Things People Love." User Testing. 4 December 2018. https://www.usertesting.com/blog/how-ideo-uses-customer-insights-to-design-innovative-products-users-love

"Identify Value Streams and ARTs." SAFe: Scaled Agile® Last updated 28 September 2019. https://www.scaledagileframework.com/identify-value-streams-and-arts/

"Introducing the Eisenhower Matrix." Eisenhower ® FTL3 Accessed 16 June 2020. https://www.eisenhower.me/eisenhower-matrix/

"Introduction to Large-Scale Scrum (LeSS)." Craig Larman. YouTube (video). Accessed 24 July 2020. https://www.youtube.com/watch?v=phOCA3myNws&t=4317s

"Kanban." *Agile Alliance* (website). Accessed 16 June 2020. https://www.agilealliance.org/glossary/kanban/

Kayser, Christopher. "The Storytelling Canvas." *Medium*. 8 August 2015. https://medium.com/@cu_ben/the-storytelling-canvas-9a5796fb39d6

Kemp, Alex. "Taiichi Ohno: Hero of the Toyota Production System." *QAD* (blog), 15 March 2018. https://blog.qad.com/2018/03/taiichi-ohno-toyota-production-system/

Kim, Daniel. "Introduction to Systems Thinking." Systems Thinker. Accessed 24 July 2020. https://thesystemsthinker.com/introduction-to-systems-thinking/

Kirsner, Scott. "The Biggest Obstacles to Innovation in Large Companies." *Harvard Business Review* (website). 30 July 2018. https://hbr.org/2018/07/the-biggest-obstacles-to-innovation-in-large-companies

Kotter, John P. "Accelerate!" *Harvard Business Review*. Nov. 2012 issue. https://hbr.org/2012/11/accelerate

Kotter, John P. *Leading Change*. Harvard Business Review Press, 2012.

Kundenzufriedenheit im IT-Outsourcing (Ferri Abolhassan, Springer Fachmedien Wiesbaden, 2014)

Laloux, Frederic. *"Reinventing Organizations: a Guide to Creating Organizations Inspired by the next Stage of Human Consciousness."* Brussels: Nelson Parker, 2014.

"The Lean Startup Methodology." The Lean Startup. Accessed 24 July 2020. http://theleanstartup.com/principles

Lencioni, Patrick. *The Five Dysfunctions of a Team: A Leadership Fable*. Jossey-Bass, 2002.

Leopold, Klaus. "Flight Levels: The Organizational Improvement Levels." LEAN*ability*. 29 April 2017. [Blog] https://www.leanability.com/en/blog-en/2017/04/flight-levels-the-organizational-improvement-levels/

Little, Jason. "What Is Lean Change Management?" Lean Change Management Accessed 24 July 2020. https://leanchange.org/lean-change-management-3/

Lu, Marcus. "50 Cognitive Biases in the Modern World." Visual Capitalist 1 Feb. 2020. https://www.visualcapitalist.com/50-cognitive-biases-in-the-modern-world/

"Magic Estimation Game: How to Do It Remotely" Inovex. Accessed 11 Oct 2020. https://www.inovex.de/blog/remote-magic-estimation-game/

Maister, David, Green Charles H. & Robert M. Galford. *The Trusted Advisor* Free Press, 2000.

Matta, Nadim F. and Ron Ashkenas. "Why Good Projects Fail Anyway." *Harvard Business Review*. Sept. 2003 Issue. https://hbr.org/2003/09/why-good-projects-fail-anyway

McGoff, Chris. *The Primes: How Any Group Can Solve Any Problem.* Wiley, 2012. Kindle.

Mehr als ein Käufer: Der Kunde, das unbekannte Wesen (Lutz von Rosenstiel und Peter Neumann), aus „Erfolgsfaktor Kundenzufriedenheit (Hansjörg Künzel, Springer Verlag Berlin Heidelberg, 2012)

Miller, Richard Dr. "Building a Successful Community of Practice."© Miller-Klein Associates, Ltd. 2006 http://miller-klein.com/wp-content/uploads/2016/12/Communities-of-Practice-Notes.pdf

Morse, John J. and Jay W. Lorsch. "Beyond Theory Y." *Harvard Business Review* (website). From the May 1970 issue. https://hbr.org/1970/05/beyond-theory-y

"Multitasking: Switching Costs." American Psychological Association. 20 March 2006. https://www.apa.org/research/action/multitask

"Network-centric organization." Wikipedia. Last modified 30 April 2020. https://en.wikipedia.org/wiki/Network-centric_organization

"The Nine Belbin Team Roles." Belbin. Accessed 24 July 2020. https://www.belbin.com/about/belbin-team-roles/

"Not Invented Here Syndrome (NIHS)." Technopedia. Last modified 1 Nov. 2012. https://www.techopedia.com/definition/3848/not-invented-here-syndrome-nihs

"PDCA." Wikipedia. Accessed 24 July 2020. https://en.wikipedia.org/wiki/PDCA

"Personality Types." 16Personalities. Accessed 24 July 2020. https://www.16personalities.com/personality-types

Pflaeging, Niels. "Agile Is Beta—keynote by Niels Pflaeging at Comelion 2019." LinkedIn SlideShare. Accessed 24 July 2020. https://www.slideshare.net/npflaeging/agile-is-beta-keynote-by-niels-pflaeging-at-comeleon-2019-zagrebhr

Pink, Daniel H. *Drive: The Surprising Truth about What Motivates Us.* Riverhead Books, 2011.

Pinola, Melanie. "Make Better Quality Decisions with the Help of this Spreadsheet." 25 January 2012. https://lifehacker.com/make-better-quality-decisions-with-the-help-of-this-spr-5879173

Playford, Brendan. "9 Challenges Hindering Innovation in Your Organization." DecipherÔ 9 June 2016. https://www.innovation-asset.com/blog/9-challenges-hindering-innovation-in-your-organization

"Productivity 101: How to Use Personal Kanban to Visualize Your Work" Lifehacker (website). Accessed 16 June 2020. https://shorturl.at/uvyY9

"The Pomodoro Technique: Do More and Have Fun with Time Management." Franceso Cirillo (website). Accessed 24 July 2020. https://francescocirillo. com/pages/pomodoro-technique

Qualitätsmanagement für Dienstleistungen (Manfred Bruhn, Springer-Verlag GmbH Deutschland, 2019)

Raedemaecker, Stefan, et al. "Lean Management or Agile? The Right Answer May Be Both." *McKinsey & Co.* 14 July 2020. https://www.mckinsey.com/ business-functions/operations/our-insights/lean-management-or-agile-the-right-answer-may-be-both

Reddy, Sudarsan. "Critical Chain Project Management Methodology and Buffers Explained." *Medium.* 27 Feb. 2019. https://medium.com/@ sudarhtc/critical-chain-project-management-methodology-and-buffers-explained-4caf3f0a2a2e

Reichert, Julia and Steven Bognar, dir. *American Factory.* 2019. Netflix Streaming.

Reklamationsmanagement – Geschenke der Kunden (Peter Diehsle), aus „Erfolgsfaktor Kundenzufriedenheit (Hansjörg Künzel, Springer Verlag Berlin Heidelberg, 2012)

Samson, Eric. "The Entrepreneur's Guide to Pay-for-Performance Consulting." March 2015. *Entrepreneur.* https://www.entrepreneur.com/article/243401

Smith, Steven M. "The Satir Change Model." 4 October 1997. Steven M. Smith (personal website). https://stevenmsmith.com/ar-satir-change-model/

Sharma, Ambika. "7 Reasons to Take Pride in Your Work or Do Something Else." Entrepreneur. 31 March 2017. https://www.entrepreneur.com/article/292231

Sloan, John. "How to Change a Culture: Lessons from NUMII." *MITSloan Management Review.* Winter 2010, vol. 51, no. 2. https://www.lean.org/Search/Documents/35.pdf

Snowden, Edward. *Permanent Record.* Metropolitan Books, 2019.

"Surviving and Thriving in an emerging Digital Media World: 4 Secrets t Success"DigitalHunters. Accessed 27 September. https://digitalhunter co.uk/surviving-andthriving in-an-emerging-digital-media-world-4-secrets to-success/

"Social Style®: The Driving Social Style." TRACOM. Accessed 24 July 202 https://tracom.com/social-style-training/model/driving-style

Sowersby, Kris. "Why Bembo Sucks." I Love Typography. Accessed 22 Sept. 2020. https://ilovetypography.com/2008/01/22/why-bembo-sucks/

"Stacey Matrix." Praxis. Accessed 22 Sept. 2020. https://www.praxisframework. org/en/library/stacey-matrix

Stern, Joshua Michael, dir. *Jobs*. 2013; Los Angeles, CA: Universal Pictures Home Entertainment, 2013. DVD.

Steve Jobs' 2005 Stanford commencement Address. 12 June 2005. Stanford News. https://news.stanford.edu/2005/06/14/jobs-061505/

Stevenson, D.H. & Starkweather, J.A. "The impact of project duration on IT project success factors." ResearchGate. January 2011. https://www. researchgate.net/publication/288354243_The_impact_of_project_ duration_on_it_project_success_factors

Strelecky, John (personal website). Accessed 24 July 2020. https://www. johnstrelecky.com/books/

Surdek, Steffan. "Why Understanding Other Perspectives Is A Key Leadership Skill." Forbes. Accessed 27 September 2020.https://www.forbes.com/sites/ forbescoachescouncil/2016/11/17/why-understandingother-perspectives- is-a-key-leadership-skill/#5db085706d20

Takeuchi, Hirotaka and Ikujiro Nonaka. "The New New Product Development Game." *Harvard Business Review* (website). From January 1986 issue. https://hbr.org/1986/01/the-new-new-product-development-game

Talbert, Robert. "GTD for Academics: Simple Trusted System." Robert Talbert (personal website). 10 March 2017. http://rtalbert.org/gtd-for-academics- simple-trusted-system/

Tavrizyan, Karine. "16 Project Management Stats You Can't Ignore." *Medium*. 11 Feb. 2019. https://medium.com/crowdbotics/hips-dont-lie-15-project- management-stats-you-can-t-ignore-6f655060ef30

"Three Key Capabilities for Agile Leaders." Business Agility Series. Accenture Solutions. https://businessagility.institute/learn/3-key-capabilities- for-agile-leaders-agileamped-podcast/#:~:text=Clarity%20of%20 purpose%2C%20control%20without,trainer%20and%20coach%2C%20P- hil%20Abernathy.Podcast.

Tolan, Josh. "The Most Efficient Interview Process Involves Your Whole Team." Spark Hire. Accessed 29 Aug. 2020. https://hr.sparkhire.com/interviewing/ efficient-interview-process-involves-whole-team/

"Topics to Talk About." *Conversation Starters World*. Accessed 24 July 2020. https://conversationstartersworld.com/topics-to-talk-about/

Ulrich, Dave. *Human Resource Champions the next Agenda for Adding Value and Delivering Results. Boston,* MA: Harvard Business School Press, 1997.

"Using the Myers-Briggs® Instrument with the DISC© Instrument." Psychometrics. https://www.psychometrics.com/wp-content/uploads/2017/08/MBTI-with-DISC.pdf

"Value Stream Coordination." SAFe: Scaled Agile® Last updated 25 June 2020. https://www.scaledagileframework.com/value-stream-coordination/

"Value Streams." SAFe: Scaled Agile® Last updated 30 June 2020. https://www.scaledagileframework.com/value-streams/

"Weekend Language." June 2016. Ben Forte (personal blog) http://1093782958.1093763584.temp.prositehosting.co.uk/weekend-language/

Weinstein, Yana. "The Cost of Task Switching." The Learning Scientists. Accessed 24 July 2020. https://www.learningscientists.org/blog/2017/7/28-1

Weiss, Dyanne. "Ideal Ratio of Managers to Staff." Azcentral. Updated 5 April 2018. https://yourbusiness.azcentral.com/ideal-ratio-managers-staff-24643.html

Welch, Jack. *Winning.* Harper Business, 2005.

"What Are Your Values? Deciding What's Most Important in Life." Mind Tools. Accessed 24 July 2020. https://www.mindtools.com/pages/article/newTED_85.htm

"What Is a Scrum Master: Learn About the Role of the Scrum Master.' Scrum.org. Accessed 24 July 2020. https://www.scrum.org/resources/what-is-a-scrum-master

White, Sarah K. "What is OKR? A goal-setting framework for thinking big." 4 September 2018. CIO. https://www.cio.com/article/3302036/okr-objectives-and-key-results-defined.html

"WHOW Matrix." Praxis. Accessed 22 Sept. 2020. https://www.praxisframework.org/en/library/whow-matrix

"Why We Hate Being Told What to Do." Pessimists Archive [podcast] Accessed 28 June 2020. https://pessimists.co/why-we-hate-being-told-what-to-do/

Willenbrock, Harald. "Eine Bank auf Speed." Brand Eins. April 2018. https://www.brandeins.de/magazine/brand-eins-wirtschaftsmagazin/2018lebensmittel/ing-diba-eine-bank-auf-speed

Wren, Hannah. "6 Tips for Improving Your Business' Customer Focus Zendesk. Last updated 18 August 2020. https://www.zendesk.de/blogwhat-is-customer-focus/

Yourdon, Edward and Larry L. Constantine. *Structured Design: Fundamentals of a Discipline of Computer Program and Systems Design*. Englewood Cliffs, NJ: Prentice Hall, 1979.

Printed in Great Britain
by Amazon